jumpstart Connections
31 Fresh Ideas to Invigorate Your Relationships

KAREN HOLFORD *and* KAREN AND RON FLOWERS

© 2006

Department of Family Ministries

General Conference of Seventh-day Adventists
12501 Old Columbia Pike
Silver Spring, MD 20904, USA
Website: http://adventistfamilyministries.org/world

Printed and distributed by
Ministerial Resource Center
12501 Old Columbia Pike
Silver Spring, MD 20904, USA
Phone: 888-771-0738
Website: http://www.ministerialassociation.com

Cover art by Dever Design

Unless designated otherwise, Scriptures are quoted from the *New International Version.*

Scriptures quoted from NIV are from the *Holy Bible, New International Version,* copyright © 1973, 1978, 1984 International Bible Society. Used by permission of Zondervan Bible Publishers.

Scriptures quoted from TEV are from the *Good News Bible Today's English Version,* Old Testament copyright © American Bible Society, 1976; New Testament copyright © American Bible Society, 1966, 1971, 1976. Used by permission.

Scriptures quoted from NKJV are from the *The New King James Version,* copyright © 1979, 1980, 1982, Thomas Nelson, Inc., Publishers.

Scriptures quoted from TM or Message are from *THE MESSAGE,* copyright © 1993, 1994, 1995. Used by permission of NavPress Publishing Group.

ISBN# 1-57847-643-9

Special thanks for Developmental Funding:

J.A. Thomas & Associates
Hospital and Physician Consulting

Table of Contents

Jumpstarts for
LIFE'S CHALLENGES

Jumpstarts for
PARENTING

Introduction

A man tells this story: While waiting to pick up a friend at the airport in Portland, Oregon, I had one of those life changing experiences that you hear other people talk about, the kind that sneaks up on you unexpectedly.

This one occurred a mere two feet away from me. Straining to locate my friend among the passengers coming off the plane through the jet way, I noticed a man coming toward me carrying two light bags. He stopped right next to me to greet his family.

First he motioned to his youngest son (maybe six years old) as he laid down his bags. They gave each other a long, loving hug. As they separated enough to look into each other's faces, I heard the father say, "It's so good to see you, son. I missed you so much!" His son smiled somewhat shyly, averted his eyes and replied softly, "Me too, Dad!"

Then the man stood up, gazed into the eyes of his oldest son (maybe nine or ten), and while cupping his son's face in his hands said, "You're already quite the young man. I love you very much, Zach!" They too hugged a most loving, tender hug.

While this was happening, a baby girl (perhaps a year old) was squirming excitedly in her mother's arms, never once taking her little eyes off her daddy. The man said, "Hi, baby girl!" as he gently took the child into his arms. He kissed her face all over and then held her close to his chest while rocking her from side to side. The little girl instantly relaxed and simply laid her head on his shoulder, motionless in pure contentment.

After a long moment, he handed his daughter to his oldest son and declared, "I've saved the best for last!" and proceeded to greet his wife affectionately. He gazed into her eyes for several seconds and then silently mouthed, "I love you so much!" They drank deeply from one another's eyes, beaming big smiles and holding hands. For an instant they reminded me of newlyweds, but the presence of three children who looked just like them pushed my thoughts in another direction.

I puzzled about it for a moment, then realized how totally engrossed I was in the wonderful display of unconditional love not more than an arm's length away from me. I suddenly felt uncomfortable, as if I was invading something sacred. Then, amazed to hear my own voice, I blurted out, "Wow! How long have you two been married?"

"Twelve years!" he replied, without breaking his gaze from his lovely wife's face.

"Well then, how long have you been away?" I asked.

The man finally turned and looked at me, still beaming that joyous smile. "Two whole days!"

Two days? I was stunned. By the intensity of the greeting, I had assumed he'd been gone at least several weeks. I know my expression betrayed me. Hoping to end my intrusion with some semblance of grace, I mumbled offhandedly, "I hope my marriage is like that after twelve years!"

The man suddenly stopped smiling. He looked me straight in the eye, and with forcefulness that burned right into my soul he told me something that left me a different person. "Don't hope, my friend, *decide!*" was all he said. Then he flashed me that wonderful smile again, shook my hand, and departed with a "God bless!" flung over his shoulder.

I was still watching that exceptional man and his precious family when my friend came off the plane and asked, "What are you looking at?"

Without hesitating, and with a curious sense of certainty, I replied: "My future!"

In those moments when life gets reduced to its essentials, family and significant relationships will always make it into the last sort. But often in the press of living, despite our best intentions, relationships are the first to be put on hold when there's overload at home and at work.

If you are looking to JumpStart connections with people you love, relationships that have been left frayed at the edges from the stresses and strains of real life, this book is for you. This book puts the best of religious and societal values into working clothes. It does not preach, but it draws on the best wisdom literature of the ages. In its pages you will find stories of people just like yourselves who know the challenges of family living first hand. Their stories are not fairytales with "and they lived happily ever after" endings. But they are stories filled with hope because the individuals and families who lived them discovered practical "doables" and took meaningful steps toward realizing their commitment to build strong relationships at home and in the wider circle.

The good news is, JumpStarting can begin with you.

jumpstarts
for Relationships

Start by Learning
Their Names 🍃

"The Lord who created you says, 'I have called you by name—you are mine.'" —Isaiah 43:1 (TEV)

It could have been any town, anyplace. The setting was a town meeting. The teenagers were into sex, alcohol and drugs, and the adults were worried. They were worried enough to throw a lot of money into prevention. The town council had brought in the best experts they could find, boasting the best resources and the most engaging props. The kids had even said "thanks" after the program. They *liked* it! But one year later, the teen pregnancy and substance abuse statistics remained the same. Despite their best efforts, it appeared little had changed.

That was the reason for the town meeting, and that was the reason for the speech. The speaker was an unlikely speechmaker. He was a lanky rancher sitting on the back row in his cowboy boots. His speech wasn't long; it was just profound. "If you want to know what I think we should do," he drawled, "I think we should start by learning their names."

In this age of worldwide communication networks and Internet search engines that can pull up personal information on anyone, it is amazing how many people feel nameless in the crowd. Researchers in a huge longitudinal study of 90,000 American adolescents have identified this nameless feeling, this lack of connectedness, as the primary factor associated with risky behavior during adolescence. Kids who feel connected to family, school, church and community are engaged in far fewer behaviors that put their long and short-term health at risk than those who do not.

Counselors listen everyday to countless lonely people who live in the midst of a sea of people but without meaningful relationships. Perhaps you are looking for a way out of this dilemma. If your people connections could use a JumpStart, then this book is for you. Like the lanky rancher's speech, these JumpStart ideas aren't complicated. But they've worked for others, and they can work for you.

In his book *Bonding: Relationships in the Image of God*, Donald Joy uses the easy-to-grasp metaphor of a trampoline to explain the importance of people connections to the overall health and well-being of human beings.[1] He says relational health is like a trampoline in good repair—it gives a lot of "bounce" to your life. Good people connections are a major source of the energy, the sense of well-being, and the happiness that makes life worth waking up to in the morning.

When the springs are broken on a trampoline or the mat has been torn from its moorings, the bounce is lost. Similarly, the relational "mat" on our inner "trampoline" must be stretched taunt if it is to function properly. Our internal relational trampolines are held taunt by the network of people in our lives who are closest to us. Researchers have concluded that in order to experience optimal health and well-being, human beings need a network of some 20-30 people in this circle of close relationships. These people can be family, friends, colleagues or even your hairdresser if a special chemistry between you has led to friendship. What counts is that you are in nearly daily contact with these people, your relationship is for the most part positive, and you know you could depend on them in an emergency, just as they could depend on you.

Put your book down for a minute and draw yourself a rectangle to represent your relational trampoline. List as many people as you can who fit the above criteria for being part of your inner support circle. If you are like most of us, you may find your list falling a bit short of the 20-30 close relationships needed for optimal health.

The good news is you can take charge of your relational trampoline. You can repair the springs and reinforce the mat until your trampoline is as good as new. You can JumpStart the relationships you have already and new ones that look promising. One by one you can build your network, and every day you can experience new "bounce" in your relationships. What's more, there's huge gratification to be found in knowing you are a spring of health and well-being for those you care about, as you take your place around their trampolines and offer them the same love and support they provide for you. JumpStarting your connections is the best way to JumpStart your life! It's never too late to begin.

Connectedness isn't all that elusive, but it does take intentionality. Life in the modern world is a whirlwind. The washer has to be fed, the computer has a nasty virus, the windows may as well be frosted glass, the cat is pregnant again, your husband is late for his meeting and the kids have filled up on peanut butter and jelly sandwiches because you're late with dinner. Where do you start to simplify? How on earth will you find energy for JumpStarting connections? You could use a JumpStart yourself, just to get through the mail!

Escaping the eye of an activity-driven whirlwind requires a paradigm shift in thinking. It calls for a deliberate change of focus from activity to people. Take a few minutes to create in your mind the best-case scenario you could imagine for yourself if you really could get your life under control. Picture the people in your network now and what it would be like to really connect with them in all the mutually satisfying ways you can think of. What would you like to be able to talk with them about? What would you like to learn from them? What would you like to do with them and for them? What kinds of things do they do that you wish you had the chance or the courage to try? What kind of sharing do you long for? Ask yourself, "What would it take to make this vision a reality?"

Real people have asked themselves these questions, and this book is about their answers. Connectedness is not about escaping into a fantasy world. It's about making the most of the everyday opportunities to demonstrate kindness, empathy, care and support in the lives of the people you care about most. It's about expanding your circle of dear ones. It's about deliberately including some people in your network that are good for you and including others because you know it will be good for them.

It's about simple things like knowing the names of your kids' friends. It's about remembering your husband has his annual evaluation with the boss this morning and telling him you'll be thinking of him as he goes out the door. People who are connected choose to make time for parties and weddings and celebrations, even though they know they will inevitably come at the "wrong" time. Connectedness means giving a person your undivided attention and picking up on feelings as well as words. It means being a trustworthy and safe friend. Connections that make a difference are warm and winsome. They make you want to come back for more.

A Kikiyu chief from East Africa, even at 80 years of age, speaks with satisfaction of the connection his mother established with him as a babe tied snugly to her back:

My early years are connected in my mind with my mother. At first she was always there: I can remember the comforting feel of her body as she carried me on her back and the smell of her skin in the hot sun. Everything came from her. When I was hungry or thirsty she would swing me round to where I could reach her full breasts; now when I shut my eyes I feel again with gratitude the sense of well-being that I had when I buried my head in their softness and drank the sweet milk that they gave. At night when there was no sun to warm me, her arms, her body, took its place; and as I grew older and more interested in other things, from my safe place on her back I could watch without fear as I wanted, and when sleep overcame me I had only to close my eyes.[2]

For our friend Harold, connecting was a learned skill. One evening he was deep into his book when his daughter Sheryl popped into the room. "Dad, do you have a minute," she inquired.

"Sure, of course honey, sit down," Harold mumbled, his eyes still on the page.

"Dad, I need to talk to you? Can you listen now?" Sheryl persisted.

"Yes!" Harold responded, a little annoyed. "Go ahead. I told you I'm listening." This time Harold lifted his eyes briefly to make eye contact, but his book remained open in his lap.

"Dad, I really need to talk to you about something important," Sheryl repeated herself for emphasis.

With this punctuation, Harold closed his book a bit impatiently, using his finger to mark his place.

"Dad, we'll talk when you can take your finger out of your book," Sheryl finished.

Connecting can be that simple! JumpStart your connections today. You'll be glad you did.

ENDNOTE

1 Donald M. Joy, *Bonding: Relationships in the Image of God* (Nappanee, Ind.: Evangel Publishing House, 1996).

2 Ashley Montagu, *Touching* (New York: Harper & Row, 1971), 79.

Appreciation:
Don't Go Home
Without It

"A word fitly spoken is like apples of gold in settings of silver."
—*Proverbs 25:11 (NKJV)*

D esmond pushed his chair back from the table. "That was a great meal, Cathy! You cooked those potatoes just the way I like them best. And the stew tasted so good! I really liked the seasonings. Not too hot, just tasty!"

Cathy smiled, "I'm glad you enjoyed your supper," she said.

Meg watched Jeff as he tried to fix her bike. It was her only transportation to work. She didn't have the time or energy to walk the five miles each way. He took off the tire, patched it, and filled it with air so he could make sure there was no evidence of further leakage in the morning. He didn't want Meg to have to push the bike home again.

"Jeff, I really want thank you for fixing my bike. And I really appreciate your taking the time to make sure that it's fixed properly." Jeff grinned. It always felt good when Meg told him how much she appreciated his help. It made him want to do his best for her. Appreciation is precious. A little bit can go a long way to make life taste better. It is one of those things of which it's hard to have too much.

Amy knew how it felt to go unappreciated. It seemed as if no one ever thanked her or said anything nice about what she did. She kept her small home tidy and tastefully decorated. She arranged the furniture and the rugs with careful thought to bringing the family together. She kept the clothes clean and mended and took care to prepare meals that were both delicious and nutritious. She worked hard at homemaking because she loved her family. She also wanted to feel good about herself as a wife and a mother. But her husband Tim never seemed to notice what she did, at least he never commented. His mother had kept a neat home, so he thought that's just what women did. Anyway, he figured, it couldn't be that much work to keep a small house tidy when Amy was at home all day with only three small children for whom to care. It wasn't as if she had that much to do.

Then one day Amy fell and broke her ankle. She had some crutches, but for weeks it was very difficult for her to keep the weight off that ankle and do her housework at the same time. She comforted herself that she could still watch the children. They were her first priority anyway. When Tim came home from work each day, he could see that Amy really needed his help to make the supper and pick up around the house. Then there was the laundry and the children's bedtime routine. He soon realized just how hard Amy worked! His words of appreciation were slow in coming, offered only in small bits at first. But the impact on his wife was truly amazing! Almost immediately it seemed Amy began to smile more. She even began to sing around the house. Before long, it seemed that the energetic and fun-loving Amy he had married began to make more regular appearances. Somehow the meals Tim had taken for granted tasted even tastier, the house seemed even more attractive and his wife more loving and beautiful than ever.

Everyone needs to feel their efforts are noticed, even rewarded occasionally. As Tim began to show his gratitude, Amy felt appreciated and valued. She was quick to realize that he probably needed to hear more affirming words too and the children as well. When Amy had more thoughtfulness coming her way, she had more to share with others.

Davy dust mopped the floor for his mother. On first examination, it looked shiny clean. But as Mom was helping him to put the furniture back where it belonged, she realized that he'd missed a bit. She had some choices about her immediate response. She could point out the bit he'd missed. She could sweep it up herself, saying nothing aloud, but by her actions making him aware he'd done a less-than-perfect job. Or, she could show appreciation for what he'd done well and just leave the dusty patch for the next time. She chose to ignore the bit of dust, emphasizing his willingness to help and the good effort he had made.

Debbie was discouraged. She tried to help around the home and did the best she could, but somehow whatever she did was never good enough. Her mother, intent on teaching her to do things right, always found something to correct. Debbie, however, read these corrections as criticism. They left her discouraged and full of feelings of resentment towards her mother.

It's so easy to focus on what's wrong rather than on what's right about someone else's efforts. It's the natural human response. But when we do this, we risk discouraging others and damaging relationships. Even when it is necessary to point out a mistake, appreciation for the effort is needed in generous proportions to the necessary correction. Ten parts affirmation to one part correction is about right, the experts say. If you can't think of ten good things to say, then just affirm what you can and forget the correction this time. We all become skilled through practice, and with each repetition, there's opportunity for improvement. In the meantime, even a small dose of gratitude and affirmation keeps people motivated to good works. Even more importantly, it helps them feel good about who they are and the contribution they are making to the family enterprise. The secret is simple. Celebrate the kinds of behaviors you want to see more often. Appreciation is never wasted. You may even share in the rewards!

Jim told the most amazing stories to his children. In the evening, they all loved to gather around the table after supper and listen to his tales, mostly about his childhood adventures. One day his son said, "Daddy, your stories are better than the stories we read at school!" Another of his children added, "Daddy, why don't you write a book. Other kids would like your stories too." Jim later reflected that without the children's affirmation, he may never have begun writing. At first he submitted his work to magazines. Then, as one by one his stories were accepted for publication, he began to dream of pulling them all together into a book. In the end, it was the income from this book that helped to pay for the children's educations.

Agneta made wonderful meals for her husband when they were first married. She put in hours of work making each one special, but he ate them without comment. Agneta longed to hear a word of appreciation or thanks, but it never came. After a year, she decided it wasn't worth the effort and began putting the simplest fare possible on the table. Within a week Sam began complaining about her cooking! Losing something often has a way of highlighting its value.

When you feel like complaining, try instead to visualize the other person behaving in positive ways, ways that would build and strengthen your relationship. Don't forget to follow their "good example" yourself. At the same time, show real appreciation for every little step the other person takes in the right direction. And while you're at it, why not write down all the things you appreciate about each of your family members. Picture them in your mind one by one. Think, "What do I most appreciate about this person? What is it about them that make me glad to be in the same family? What efforts on their part deserve a word of thanks? What unique gifts and joys do they bring to this family that I wouldn't want to live without?" After making your lists, think of all kinds of ways you could show your appreciation.

Watch for opportunities to say things like, "I like the way you do your hair. It really suits your face." "It's wonderful the way you cook rice. You make it taste so good." "Thank you for cleaning the shoes. It's so nice to have them ready to wear in the morning." Maybe you could write a little note of appreciation and tuck it in a place where your spouse or child will find it. Or perhaps you might be more intentional about putting your own things away to show how much you appreciate an attractive home. Appreciation is like a glass of water on a hot day. It refreshes everyone and keeps them energized. Without it, people wilt like flowers in the heat.

Is there someone close to you who's thirsty for appreciation? Why not start by noticing the effort they are putting into making your life more interesting, more comfortable, more fun. A word of thanks each day is a great thing to say!

Half the Work,
Double the Pleasure

"My lover spoke and said to me, 'Arise, my darling, my beautiful one, and come with me. See! The winter is past; the rains are over and gone. . . . Arise, come, my darling; my beautiful one, come with me.'" —*Song of Songs 2:10-13*

Joel and Megan moved into the city to find work. Housing was very expensive there. The only way they could afford a place was to find an old apartment that needed lots of improvement. Every day after work and during all their free time on the weekends, they were busy tearing out old fittings, repairing walls, scrubbing rust from old sinks and tubs, sanding and refinishing woodwork, and decorating with furniture from the second hand shop. It was a big project. But as they worked they chatted, listened to the radio, and talked about their ideas and dreams for their new home. They each brought their unique talents to the project and helped the other learn new skills. Sure, there were times when they disagreed about how something should be done, and plenty of times they got frustrated with each other and with their project. But as their home began to take new shape, so did their relationship.

"We thought we were best friends before we tackled the apartment, but we are closer now than ever! It feels so good to walk into our home and know it's truly ours, something we created together," says Megan.

"We learned a lot," adds Joel, "I never knew there was so much to know! I am amazed at how good Megan is at some things. And it's great to know that between us we can probably handle almost any household emergency."

Doing things together is an important part of building a strong relationship and growing closer. Think of the benefits Joel and Megan would have lost if Joel had tackled the refurbishing all on his own. He could easily have felt resentful toward Megan for not helping, while she may have become annoyed that the project took so long. Joel might have felt that he "owned" the project and been unwilling to give Megan a say in what was being done. She could have grown frustrated because Joel was so absorbed in *his* project that he wasn't spending enough time with her. By the time their home was finished, Joel and Megan could easily have found themselves drifting apart.

Doing things together says "I need you. I value your opinion. I affirm your giftedness and skills. I want us to be in this together." Not only couples, but parents and children, even friends, feel good when they know that somebody desires their input and involvement. When working alone, it's easy to get disheartened, lose interest, feel overburdened and even give up. But when we share a challenging task with someone else, we often find we can stick at it a bit longer. When one gets tired or discouraged, the other person can help them stay with the project until things get easier.

Dave learned to play the violin along with his five-year-old son Jason. They worked toward music exams together, and once or twice, Jason even made better scores than his dad! They had much more fun practicing together than they would have had separately.

Kelly wanted to learn Spanish, but she didn't want to go to the evening classes by herself. So her friend Anna joined her. They called each other every day and agreed to speak only Spanish on the phone. They tested each other and challenged one another to friendly competition. At the end of the course, they treated themselves to a trip abroad where they could practice their new skills in a real-world setting.

Ben's bedroom was always a mess. It was so bad that his family had even threatened to fence it off with hazard warning tape. No one was sure what was under his bed, but it was rumored that sometimes it moved! Even his mom wouldn't go into his room anymore. The only part of the room that anyone could describe as clean was the ceiling. No matter how often he was told, "You absolutely must clean up your room, Ben!" it just didn't happen.

One day his dad asked him why he never cleaned his room. Ben hung his head. "I don't know how, Dad. Nobody's ever shown me what to do." Dad decided to offer to help Ben tackle his room. They both had a good laugh when Dad provided rubber gloves and dust masks as they set to work. Dad showed Ben how to hang his pants and shirts in one part of his closet and his jackets in another. He demonstrated how he folded his own underwear and socks to conserve drawer space. Together they organized Ben's storage areas and decided what to throw out and what to keep. As a finishing touch, Dad took his son out to buy some new posters. Ben was so pleased with his room makeover. It sure was easier—and much more fun—working together with Dad than it had been sitting in the middle of all his mess and not knowing where to start.

Working together is important, but nothing puts energy back into a tired, boring or even struggling relationship than fun together. One family tells funny stories about their experiences each day when they sit down to eat supper. Matthew and Lynne make kites together. She sews amazing brightly-colored kites from the patterns Matthew designs. After they have assembled all the parts, they go out to the hills to test-fly their creations! If you've ever tried to fly a kite on your own, you'll know that it's always a good idea to have someone else along to give you a hand. Some of their kites have won prizes. They've even been able to sell some of their work.

For Tim and Tina, New Year's Eve has become an occasion for making a list of all the things they'd like to do together in the coming year. Each month they take turns choosing something from the other person's list. Even if it's not something they both like, they try to go along cheerfully for the other person's sake. Tim says, "I've learned about quilting, and Tina's even tried go-kart racing. I'd definitely be the poorer, in terms of life experience, if I didn't have Tina as my partner."

Tina adds, "I like having something to look forward to each month. It kind of makes everything else in our lives more tolerable. We always know it won't be long before we enjoy our next treat. Sometimes our fun time can be as simple as a walk in the park with bread for the ducks, or taking a blanket and a hot drink into a field at night to watch for shooting stars. It doesn't have to cost anything to make a very special memory."

Often it is self-reliance that stops us doing from doing more things together. It's the attitude, "I can make it on my own. I don't need you or anybody else." Many people with this attitude are really shaky inside about whether others like them and want to do things with them. It's easier to put on a front of self-sufficiency than it is to risk being rejected and hurt. In the past, families and communities had to work together for their own survival. But today, many cultures convey the message that "real" men and women are big and strong and independent, in need of no one else's support.

People who put up this front might be afraid that if they work on a project with you, you'll reject their ideas, so it's safer to work alone. They might be afraid that if they play tennis with you, you'll be better than they are, and they'll feel like a failure. Maybe they just want to be in control and have it all their own way without considering what you would like. They may just think that it will be quicker if they do things on their own. But these kinds of attitudes send the hidden message, "I don't need you," and create a distancing in a relationship.

Dan says, "We used to draw up a list of things that needed doing around the house and divide them between us to get them done. We'd each struggle with some of our jobs and often get frustrated. Now we share lots of jobs, helping each other wherever we can, learning from each other and feeling much less frustrated and alone. When we accomplish something really tough together, then we celebrate big time."

Does someone need your help today? Is someone in your family circle longing to enjoy the fun side of you? Don't go it alone. No matter what the challenge, consider sharing the experience. It may turn out to be one of those half the work, double the pleasure experiences after all.

Investments
That Count

"Freely you have received, freely give." —*Matthew 10:8*

Jorge could trace kidney disease through his family tree like a dark thread. It had always been a bit of a worry, but nothing that he couldn't manage with regular medical checkups and medications, that is until his body clock turned over to the big 5-0. Suddenly Jorge began experiencing problems he had only heard his relatives talk about. He remembered all too well the day his own father had started dialysis treatments. He didn't want to think about the ever increasing frequency and discomfort of his dad's medical regimen, let alone the complications that finally took his father's life.

It wasn't long after his 50th birthday that Jorge's own kidney function decreased drastically to levels that made dialysis treatment an imminent reality. As Jorge sat in the doctor's office with his wife Josie, they both struggled to come to grips with the implications of what the specialist was telling them: "The only other good treatment option available at the present time is a kidney transplant," she explained. "If you wish to pursue this option, we will put you on the list immediately. I must tell you, however, that it usually takes at least four years for a donor match to be found." Meanwhile, she recommended that Jorge begin dialysis immediately. The couple looked at one another in disbelief. Of course they would pursue any option that would offer the best quality of life possible. But four years! It seemed like an eternity.

Then Josie spoke. "Could I be tested to see if I'm a match?" she inquired, reaching over to quiet her husband's protests by placing her hands gently over his. Smiling warmly at Josie for her unselfish gesture, the doctor agreed that, of course, she could be tested. But so as not to raise false hopes of a quick solution, the physician was quick to add that, unfortunately, the chances of a match being found between spouses was not very good at all.

Sometimes however, despite the odds, the unlikely happens. Josie was found to be a match, and a near perfect one at that. Many tests later, the surgery was scheduled, and Jorge and Josie found themselves waking up in side-by-side beds in the hospital. "So far, so good," they sent out word to those who had been praying for them and wishing them well. "Jorge is in the next bed reading his 'new owner's manual,'" quipped Josie, her infectious sense of humor very much alive.

Most marriage partners don't face circumstances that occasion giving to one other in such remarkable ways. But in the day to day, there are many less dramatic opportunities to strengthen your relationship by giving of oneself in little ways that send the same important message: "I love you and cherish you." When, on the other hand, a person draws heavily on a partner, while seldom if ever giving in return, the relationship is inevitably weakened. Without attention, relational reserves are eventually depleted, with nothing to replenish them.

Legend has it that in long ago medieval times, the locals in one village all worked together to build a strong castle to protect them from their enemies. But after many years, the threat of an attack seemed remote, and the castle was no longer a focal point of village life. No one really owned the castle or felt responsible to look after it. It just was part of the landscape of a bygone era that everyone took for granted.

One day a villager needed some stones to mend his cottage. He happened on the old castle wall, already crumbling in disrepair. It was a convenient source of the needed materials, so he and his family helped themselves. A neighbor passing by asked him what he thought he was doing. The man was quick to defend his actions. "All the villagers helped to build this castle, so it belongs to all of us. The way I see it, I'm just taking my bit."

Later, when the same neighbor needed to mend the wall around his chickens, he remembered the castle wall. It seemed so much easier to help himself to these stones than to haul rocks from the hills. So the next day he too went to the castle and carried away "his share" of the old stones. Soon, whenever any of the villagers needed stones for a job, they would just go over to the castle and take whatever they wanted.

Then, as the story goes, a civil war broke out and the village was once again under immanent threat. "The soldiers are coming!" a cry went forth one afternoon. "Quick! Get into the castle! We'll be safe there." The villagers gathered their belongings and went up to the castle, but realized to their dismay that their castle couldn't save them any more. They had used the makings of its strong stone wall to build and do repairs for many years.

Now there was nothing left to protect them from the approaching enemy forces. They had taken from their refuge, but they had put nothing back.

Mental health professionals calculate that to be healthy, people need a network of 30 or so close friends, family and associates with whom they have frequent and positive contact. These are the people they could count on to be there for them in an emergency. Few can honestly say that their networks of such people are full to overflowing. Most of us know from personal experience how hard it is to put aside your own agenda and give of your time and energy in the interest of relationship building. But such investments pay large dividends.

Who would love to have some of your time and attention today? Maybe your child needs help with his science project. Maybe your wife could use a weekend free of family responsibilities to enjoy her friends and recharge her batteries. Maybe your husband would really like you to try cycling or jogging with him, or at least to be there to cheer him on when he competes. Maybe there are friends who have stopped inviting you over because you're never available, but who would love to join you for a simple picnic over the weekend just to catch up on your lives.

Giving, just for the sake of giving, often has a way of coming back to you in unexpected ways. Kim washed the car for Chris. It made her happy that evening as she watched him relax enough to enjoy a game with the children. Becky volunteered to cook supper so that her mom could finish a new dress she was making for herself. When Becky heard a neighbor compliment her mom on how nice she looked in her new dress, Becky said it felt better than receiving the compliment herself.

Giving generally generates a warm response on the part of the receiver too. Lyndon offered to help Tracy wash the windows because he knew she felt overwhelmed by such big jobs and found it hard to tackle them alone. Lyndon commented later, as they sat together admiring their shining windows in the evening sun, that just seeing her smile was worth every bit of the hard work

Surprises are wonderful, too! Dave saw Lucy admiring a dress in a catalog one day, so he ordered it and had it sent it to her office. Ron arranged for friends to care for the children, secretly packed a suitcase for his wife, and whisked her off on a surprise weekend holiday straight from work on Friday. Julie loved to hear her husband laugh. So for weeks she collected cartoons from newspapers, magazines and anywhere else she could find them. The scrapbook she made for him provided a huge dose of humor for the whole family whenever it was needed. Jon's wife had to be away on business. He found a poem on a card in a shop that expressed his feelings of love. He copied it in his own hand, sealed it in an envelope, and arranged with a woman who would be traveling with her to place his love gift on her hotel pillow.

One husband made a lamp for his wife from a lovely piece of cedar and gave it to her with a note that read, "You light up my life!" Another carved a heart for his beloved from olive wood. It was beautifully smooth and nestled perfectly in her hand. She kept it in her pocket as a reminder of her husband's love. Just picking up on the interests of a family member and giving a token gift that would please them—a plant for the garden, a birdfeeder, a new journal they'd enjoy—makes a big difference in relationships. Gifts don't have to be big or expensive to say "I was thinking about you with love!" Where will you begin to top up your relationships with thoughtful giving?

It's Good to be Me

"I will give up whole nations to save your life, because you are precious to me and because I love you and give you honor."
—Isaiah 43:4 (TEV)

Oliver felt good. His mom had given him a big hug that morning when he awoke. He had been able to help his dad paint the fence around the backyard over the weekend. Dad said he did a very good job. His teacher had given him a good mark for his math homework, and he had scored a big goal when he played football with his friends. So there was Oliver, running home from school full of good feelings—until he accidentally bumped into a neighbor with an armload of bags and papers. Some of the man's papers scattered across the lawn. Oliver stopped to help and to apologize, but before he could say anything, the angry neighbor yelled, "You stupid boy! You are so clumsy! Can't you do anything right?"

Oliver's good feelings evaporated. He hadn't meant to bump into the man; it was an accident. But his angry words shattered Oliver's happy world. Fortunately, Oliver had caring parents and a kind teacher who understood the need for children and adults to feel good about who they are. In time, their understanding and encouragement helped to restore his joy and confidence.

Why is a sense of self-worth so important? Appropriate feelings of self-worth contribute to a person's self-respect, confidence, dignity and overall sense of well-being. By contrast, people who don't feel good about themselves are often inhibited by feelings of insecurity, fear and lack of confidence. Children who feel good about themselves are more likely to be able to stand up for what they believe to be right. They will be better equipped to live by their values in the face of peer and media pressure to do otherwise. A confident and secure child will also be able to relate better to others and to achieve their potential in school. Most importantly, these children are much more likely to be successful as adults and to treat others with the respect and love that they have experienced. Whole communities benefit when children are brought up with these positive experiences. There is better health, less crime, more creativity and excellence in every area of life, more caring for one another and shared happiness.

As John Powell concludes in his book *The Secret of Staying in Love*:

> There is one need so fundamental and so essential that if it is met, everything else will almost certainly harmonize in a general sense of well-being. When this need is properly nourished, the whole human organism will be healthy and the person will be happy. This need is *a true and deep love of self, a genuine and joyful self-acceptance, an authentic self-esteem*, which result in *an interior sense of celebration*: "It's good to be me. . . . I'm very happy to be me!"[1]

When was the last time you felt happy being just who you are? There are so many things that work against such an inner celebration. Every society has unwritten criteria against which the worth of each person is measured. While there are some variations from place to place on how these standards are defined, there are some common denominators. In many places, sons are favored over daughters. Personal characteristics such as good looks, intelligence, wealth, and extraordinary talent also weigh in on the positive side of the personal value scale. If you are born with the "right" package, or somehow manage to put enough of it together, you have a good chance of being included as part of the in-crowd. Without it, you may well be relegated, by society at least, to the sidelines. Too many experiences like Oliver's with the neighbor can also affect a person profoundly. From the time a child is born they are watching, gathering data from everywhere about how others view them. The all-important question, "Am I a valuable person?" is always in their minds.

People struggle with a sense of personal worth whenever the person they portray themselves to be on the outside is not the same as the person they know themselves to be on the inside. This can happen when a person chooses to live a lifestyle that is not in keeping with the values they claim to uphold. It can also happen when other people's expectations of a person are unrealistic. The person may try very hard to measure up, but become discouraged when, despite their best efforts, they seem never to be good enough. When the family or community is critical and unaccepting, or when there is little forgiveness and encouragement for personal growth, people often feel they must pretend to be something they are not. But instead of leaving the person with a stronger sense of their value, this dissonance robs them of the satisfaction of knowing that just being themselves is enough to secure their place in the family and community.

Building worth in others begins with the understanding that all human beings are valuable and deserve to be treated with dignity and respect just because they are. In other words, human worth is intrinsic. It is not based on achievement, performance or any other criteria a family or society might impose. For many people, this truth is rooted in the biblical teaching that human beings are the handiwork of a Creator God.

Our friend Ron was once in deep in conversation with a friend. He started to step backward, unaware that he was about to step on the toes of a very little girl. A voice called out to stop him: "Be careful, Ron. There's a person behind you!" Turning to apologize to what he expected to be another adult, Ron was surprised to find a very little person looking up at him. He couldn't help but reflect how someone's calling this child a "person" had made him see her through new glasses and think more about the respect due her. He would never again look at children in quite the same way.

Spending time with each person in the family and together as a family is one of the best ways to convey how much you treasure each one and value your life together. One executive placed his business calendar on the dinner table regularly and gave each family member a chance to "make an appointment" with him, as well as appointments for them to be together as a family. He was a corporate vice-president, and there were many demands on his time. But he promised his family that he would keep their appointments as faithfully as he kept those related to his business.

The test came several weeks later when the chairman of the board announced an emergency board meeting for the next afternoon when the family had scheduled an afternoon at the beach. This executive father looked at his calendar, took a deep breath, and told the board chairman that he had a prior engagement that could not be changed. The following afternoon found the family together at the beach. The next day back at the office, one of his colleagues came by his desk and chided, "Was that you I saw playing ball on the beach late yesterday afternoon? I thought you said you had an appointment!"

"I did," the executive replied. "One of the most important appointments on my calendar!"

Hurtful communication has profound effects on feelings of self-worth. The words that we say and the nonverbal messages that we convey stay in people's minds and repeat themselves over and over, long after we may have forgotten the language or the hurtful manner in which it was spoken. As poet Will Carleton put it, "Boys flying kites haul in their white-winged birds; you can't do that when you're flying words." Think back to your own childhood. Are there words that still ring in your ears? Are they positive or negative words? What messages played a large role in shaping your feelings about yourself? What messages bear repeating in the ears of your children and family members? What messages will you decide to "dam up" with your generation, so their hurtfulness will not flow to the generations after you—your children and grandchildren?

Contrary to popular belief, praise does not make children proud. It makes them confident and eager to try new things. The wise parent or partner doesn't notice the little imperfections, only the willing heart and the smiling face of the loved one who has tried so hard to please them! Look for the best in your family, and let them know you've found it. Smile at them! A smile can be sunshine enough for an entire day for someone in your family.

Take a few minutes today to picture each one of your family members in your mind. How will you treat them to best convey the high esteem in which you hold them and how much you cherish them as a person?

ENDNOTE

1 John Powell, *The Secret of Staying in Love* (Niles, IL: Argus Communications, 1974), 13.

Laughter Really Is
Good Medicine

"A cheerful heart is good medicine." —*Proverbs 17:22*

Susan's dad's opening line at the dinner table was always, "Have you heard the one about . . . ?" During their teen years, you might well have caught Susan and her brothers rolling their eyes and mouthing the words "Number 24" behind their hands as he began. They were smiling about the numbering system they had devised in good fun for Dad's oft repeated jokes. Dad knew the joke was on him, since one of his favorites was about the old men sitting around the village square who had heard one another's jokes so many times they had given them all numbers. The punch line came after one poor joker called out "Number 17!" and no one laughed. "Why is nobody laughing?" a newcomer asked. "Well, you know how it is," an old timer replied. "Some people just can't tell a joke!"

Suffice it to say that today Susan's memories of home are filled with laughter, and she can pull up a funny story for most any occasion. Her father died several years ago now, but whenever a holiday meal brings the family together, someone will likely begin, "Have you heard the one about . . . ." Warm memories of Dad always prevail.

There are funny people in the world. People who are quick-witted, droll and full of one-liners to make you laugh. Most of us, however, are not born comedians. Nevertheless, we like to laugh and appreciate those who can help us see the humor in life around us. Humor is one of the common elements healthy families share. It eases them over the rough spots and puts a smile into everyday living side by side.

Dan's family loved to watch sports on TV. Their favorite show was a replay of the sports "bloopers" of the week at the end of the Sunday evening news. The footage featured the likes of ball players letting a ball drop in the midst of them when any one of them could have caught it. Or a player accidentally scoring in his own net. Or a golfer missing an incredibly easy putt. Watching the humorous summary of the week's games became a family ritual. No one wanted to miss the few minutes of reliving the games and laughing again at some plays that were truly unbelievable! Once the boys picked up on this theme for a family reunion and put together their own blooper show from home videos. Laughing at themselves as a family provided some of the reunion's most unforgettable moments.

Life can be so serious and full of stress that we sometimes miss how funny some things that just happen really are. A common thread that runs through healthy families is an ability to see the funny side. Madge has this marvelous knack. When one of her daughters got married, Madge wanted to look her very best—and more than that, she wanted to look quite proper. She decided to splurge and order a new hat at the haberdashery. The hat was delayed in coming and arrived just before the wedding. To Madge's dismay, the fit was not quite right, but there was no time now for adjustments.

The wedding was splendid, but in the heat of the afternoon, Madge was having more and more difficulty keeping the hat from sliding down on her forehead. Standing in the foyer of the church just after the service, her eyes happened to fall on the vicar's wastebasket. It was full to the brim with scrap paper, and therein she saw the solution to her problem. Slipping around the corner, she quickly removed her hat, stuffed it full of the vicar's discarded paperwork, and put it back on her head. Holding her head high, she then made her way across the green to the reception in the church hall. Unfortunately, a sudden gust of wind caught the brim of her hat. Off it flew, and with it, the contents of the wastebasket scattered across the lawn. Looking quickly around, she determined to her relief that she was alone. Quickly she gathered the paper stuffings and pushed them back into her hat. She was just adjusting it back onto her head when she was suddenly startled by a stately woman standing to the side, clearly amused by the whole scene. Madge felt a flush of embarrassment color her cheeks when she recognized the woman as a member of the groom's family. But she did not have to worry long. With a chuckle and a wink, the stately woman took her arm and whispered, "That was a truly marvelous solution! But we'll keep this laugh between us."

The kind of humor that brings families together is humor that laughs "with" rather than "at" family members. There is nothing more painful than finding oneself the brunt of another's jokes and put downs. This is really not humorous at all. To make jokes at the expense of another drives a wedge deep into the heart of a relationship. It is usually not helpful to make jokes when another is in pain. Humor can be a wonderful antidote for discouragement and despair in a family, but only when everyone is ready to laugh—and laugh together.

Children are a marvelous source of humor in families. Listen in on their conversations. Write down the funny sayings and happenings of every day. Childhood passes so quickly and memories do fade. Your journal will be worth its weight in gold when you're 50. Along the way, it will make great reading on a rainy day. If you have any doubts about the natural humor of little people, enjoy the following childish takes on the meaning of love circulating anonymously around the Internet:

Manuel (age 8): "When you're in love, I think you're supposed to get shot with an arrow or something, but the rest of it isn't supposed to be so painful!"

Mae (age 9): "No one is sure why it happens, but I think it has something to do with how you smell. That's why perfume and deodorant are so popular!"

Dave (age 8): "Love will find you, even if you are trying to hide from it. I've been trying to hide from it since I was five, but the girls keep finding me."

Alonso (age 9): "If you want someone to love you, don't wear your smelly green sneakers. You might get attention, but attention isn't the same thing as love!"

Bart (age 9): "One way to get a girl to love you is to take her out to eat. Make sure the place is really nice and the food is really good. Fish and chips usually work for me!"

Raj (age 8): "If you want your love to last, be a good kisser. It might make your wife forget that you forgot to take out the trash again!"

Some temperaments seem to excel in the humor department. There are the quiet funny types who don't say much, and what they do say, they say with an expressionless face. It's only fifteen minutes later that you wake up to the fact that what they said was really hilarious. Then there are the exuberant, outgoing, life-of-the-party sorts who love to tell stories, and the more their stories are appreciated, the better they get. As one woman of this genre put it, "Who'd want to pass on a dull story!" Florence Littauer, in her book *Personality Plus*,[1] tells of one such woman wound up by the rapt attention and response of a large group of friends gathered around her at a party. She told of a recent vacation to offshore islands. She went into amazing detail about the boat trip, the roughness of the seas, the seasickness of passengers, and on and on. When she finally finished her story with great fanfare, it was her quiet husband who provided its best line. He said only two words: "We flew!"

One family keeps a file they call "Just for Laughs." When they read something funny, or pick up a funny e-mail from a friend, they put a copy in there. You never know when such a file might come in handy. One summer when the family made a cross-country trip by car, someone thought to bring the folder. It provided more than an hour of entertainment, memories and laughter as they took turns drawing from its contents and reading to one another. More than once a family member was seen sharing the file with a friend who needed a lift or just fingering through it to enjoy a few laughs.

Laughter is infectious. If someone gets started, it's almost impossible to resist joining in. Try it! It will add years to your life! They even say it burns as many calories as exercise.

ENDNOTE

1 Florence Littauer, *Personality Plus* (Old Tappan, NJ: Fleming H. Revell, 1982).

Memory
Makers

"Every time you cross my mind, I break out in exclamations of thanks to God."—Philippians 1:3 (TM)

It had been hard for Andrea to get the day off work for her son's school sports day. In the end, she had to take the day as unpaid leave. She would miss the money, but Tim had asked her to come. She felt it was important to be there. He had signed up to compete in six events. As the day progressed, she was there to see him win again and again. She had no idea he was such a talented athlete. At the end of the day, her buttons were bursting as the principal presented him with the coveted all-school sports medal. Certainly being there to cheer him on and to share in his success was worth far more to Andrea than a day's wages! Even if Tim had lost every contest, the day would have been just as precious. In fact, her presence may have been even more important to Tim if he'd had a disappointing time. It was a memory that would last a lifetime.

Shared memories strengthen relationships and bring us closer to each other, especially when the memories have lots of positive feelings attached to them. Molly reached for her camera as she watched Becky topple over into the soft grass. As she snapped her picture, her toddler was flat on her back, feet in the air, boisterously giggling to herself. Only a moment before, she had been chasing a fluttering butterfly, arms outstretched. Molly didn't have that many memories of fun times with her family growing up. Her parents saw that she had basics like food, clothes and a good education, but work came before play in their ethic. They seldom got around to recreation. Molly wanted things to be different for her children. She wanted their memories to be brightly colored with laughter, adventure and warmth. Chasing butterflies and rolling in soft grass were just the beginning.

Carol read in a book that parents have a very special window of opportunity for bonding with their children in preadolescence. Her eleven-year-old son Todd had a science fair coming up, so she volunteered to team up with him on a project. Since family friends had just given Todd his first pair of binoculars for his birthday, he decided to do a bird feeding experiment.

Todd found a book of birdfeeder designs in the library, and with some technical help from Dad, he and his mom built the feeders they would need. They read up on some of the birds they hoped to attract and devised their various experiments. They set up their observation platform outside Todd's bedroom window. Every morning they watched to see which birds would come and the food choices they preferred. They made careful field notes and compared their results with the findings of others. Todd wrote his report, and together he and Carol made three beautiful posters describing the experiment. Today, Todd is a doctoral student in biology and an avid birder with a life list of over 1,000 birds. He and Carol just made the trip of a lifetime to bird together for three days in the rainforests of Costa Rica. Bond they did, indeed!

There's no end to the ideas for memory making. Nikki and James can hardly wait for Friday night to come so they can open the special Kid's Drawer that their mother stocks for them. It's a drawer that's open for only 24 hours a week—from sundown on Friday to sundown on Saturday. Every week there's a special surprise. One week it was full of dress-up clothes for a family drama production. Last winter there were hooked rug kits with nature designs for the whole family. Once the drawer produced two new fish for the aquarium. Sometimes there are stacks of books from the library and the whole family cuddles under quilts in the family room for an evening of stories. The best thing about Friday night is their parents have time!

The Hayward family plays hide-and-seek in their house in the dark. The rules are that one person hides and the rest look. When you find the person who's hiding, you quietly get in with them wherever they are and wait for the rest to find you both. Usually the growing group of "finders" end up giving themselves away with laughter. Everybody remembers the night the smallest Hayward hid herself so well no one could find her. After several minutes, a little voice was heard in the darkness. "Will somebody please find me! I don't like being in here by myself."

Doug and Estelle marked their wedding anniversary last year by dressing up in their wedding clothes and serving a special dinner to their children. They repeated their marriage vows and told the children stories about special times in their life together. They want their children to know how much they love each other and that they intend to make their marriage work.

Eric and Moira take a boat out on the river for a picnic with their children at the same time each year. As the children get older, they are initiated into the family rowing crew. Everyone looks forward to what they have affectionately dubbed "Boat Day."

Jim built a tree house that is the envy of the neighborhood. Once the whole family is inside and the door is closed, no one else can get in because the door becomes the floor! Closing the door is getting a bit more tricky now because everyone's getting bigger, but they still have their weekly family meetings there.

The Wallace family celebrates half-birthdays with a tiny gift and cupcakes.

Zak planted a tree when his son was born. The tree was exactly as tall as Baby Bryan was long. Each year Zak takes a picture of his son next to the tree. They are making a special book to show how they have both grown. Each year Zak also writes his son a letter telling him about all the special memories he has of him throughout the year. These go into the book too, with the birthday letter opposite the tree photo.

In some countries, the winter evenings are dark and long and cold. One family warms up their hearts and their kitchen baking cookies. They each take a turn finding a new cookie recipe. Then they all help to make the cookies and share them with their neighbors while they are still warm from the oven.

Andy's grandma has a friend who travels all over the world for her work. She brings back coins from all the different countries she visits. Andy and his grandma have made a wonderful book with coins and information from the Internet about each of the countries, including a color printout of the country's flag. Looking at the thick book they have made is almost as much fun as making it in the first place.

Special memories give a family a sense of close identity. Together you share something unique. Even when you are miles away from each other, traditions that you once shared remind you of the good times you've had. Ewan was a long way from home studying at university. He missed his family and thought fondly of the night each week that his family came together for a candlelight soup supper and games. Ewan decided to start the tradition of candlelight game nights in his dorm room. He had no way to serve soup, so he served fruit instead. He told his friends about his family's tradition, and soon he wasn't so lonely any more. His idea was so popular that the candlelit game night had to move to a bigger room. It wasn't long before it became an established dormitory tradition.

The kids in the Harris family are firm believers in the old adage, "Laughter is the best medicine." Doctors have confirmed that seriously ill people have literally laughed themselves better! At the Harris's, family members share funny stories, cartoons, jokes and crazy ideas by e-mail, in coat pockets and on the family refrigerator door.

Sunday night is 'Tickle Fight Night' in the Gilbert home. Once all the children are bathed and ready for bed, they all have a tickle fight. The rules are that you must "tickle gently," and you have to stop when someone asks you to stop. That way, no-one gets too overwhelmed by the tickles or hurt in the excitement.

Graham remembers music night in his house. Once a week the family would bring out all the musical instruments they could find, and they'd play music together. Sometimes they would play songs that everyone knew, and sometimes they would make them up as they went along. Even the smallest children could join in with shaker instruments or by banging on the bottom of a pan.

Save the memories, not only in your own minds, but in as many other ways as you can! Take photographs. Keep a diary of special events. Make scrapbooks and collages of tickets, menus, pressed flowers and feathers or whatever, to remind you of special times together. Memories are the ties that bind forever!

The Gift that
Returns to You

"Show proper respect to everyone." —1 Peter 2:17

As the story goes, Johnny Lingo worked as a trader between tropical islands. He fell in love with a young girl on his island, a girl nobody wanted. In their tradition, the bridegroom must bargain with the father of the bride-to-be, offering him cows for the hand of his beloved. The prettier and more talented the bride, the more cows it would take to finalize the arrangements. In fact, the number of cows exchanged for her in betrothal became the village measuring stick for the worth of a woman.

When Johnny sought Mahanna for his bride, her father joked that his daughter was so ugly and shy he had always expected to have to *give* her future husband several cows just to be rid of her. Villagers agreed that Johnny could have arranged his marriage to Mahanna for the price of one old cow. Imagine the shock waves that reverberated through the region when, in a grand public ceremony, Johnny offered Mahanna's father eight cows for his daughter. The old man was at first struck dumb with astonishment. Later he concluded Johnny must be stupid. No one in the history of the island had ever paid eight cows for a wife, and for Mahanna! At the wedding feast, Johnny felt Mahanna's pain as she once again became the object of cruel jokes and laughter. In the midst of the revelry, he silently whisked her away on a honeymoon journey that was to last many months.

When Johnny returned, a beautiful and graceful woman was on his arm. His father-in-law was immediately concerned. What had happened to Mahanna? The only logical conclusion he could reach was that Johnny had obviously realized she wasn't worth having after all. Soon the whole island turned out to see Johnny's new wife. It took some time for the islanders to recognize she was indeed Mahanna. What a transformation! She was beyond a doubt the most beautiful woman on the island. Worth ten cows at least!

Johnny knew the transformational power of love in action. When he offered eight cows for Mahanna, he demonstrated how valuable she was in his eyes. When the other women boasted about how many cows their husbands paid for them, none could ever say she was worth more than Mahanna. But this extravagant gesture was only the beginning. In the months they spent away, Johnny demonstrated his love in a myriad of ways, shielding her from ridicule, affirming her strengths, encouraging her in moments of self doubt. Slowly she began to feel good about herself and blossomed into the beautiful person he always knew she was inside.

When we respect someone, we demonstrate the value and worth we place upon them. Human beings often offer more respect to those in authority, or to those with lots of money and power, than we do to people without such distinctions. But the truth is that every individual is of equal value. Christians believe each person is precious, unique and of priceless worth because they are God's creation and because Jesus died to save them. A starving child, a person with AIDS, a dying old lady or the poorest beggar are as deserving of respect as a president, an Olympic gold medalist or a corporate executive.

Respect cannot be demanded. It is returned. Stephen and Michael were both leaders in a youth group. Stephen would raise his voice and demand that the young people respect him. Michael treated each teen as if they were uniquely special and valuable. It should come as no surprise that it was Michael who gained the most respect.

Joe believed that as husband and father he had the authority to insist that his family respond to his commands without question. He was not interested in his wife's viewpoint. If his children disobeyed him, he would punish them harshly. Open ridicule was forthcoming whenever anyone in the family made a mistake. Needless to say, home wasn't a happy place to be when Joe was there. The children were quietly rebellious. His wife endured. They treated him respectfully as their father, but in their hearts they had no respect for him at all. Real respect comes from the mutual exchange of esteem and dignity in a relationship. Treating others with respect is a good investment. The more respect we show to our marriage partners, our children, our parents, our siblings, the more respect will be shown to us.

Respect is much more than behaving politely and extending common courtesies, as important as these are. Here a few practical ideas:

Involve others in decision-making. If you are making a decision that will affect someone else, ask them for their ideas and input into the decision. Think of this when you want to invite others home for a meal, take a trip, commit yourself to a project, distribute household chores, make an important parenting decision. First listen to the other person's perspective and accommodate their wishes if you can. If you can't, see if you can agree together on a solution that meets both their needs and your own. Let everyone know that their ideas are important to you.

Allow others to express an opinion. Respect allows for opinions different from your own. Respect helps a person discern between viewpoints that are merely different from one's own and beliefs and behaviors that are morally wrong. When there is respect in a relationship, each can offer the other opportunity to calmly and politely put their views across. Respect requires a willingness to consider differing perspectives.

Respect the property of others. Respectful people ask the rightful owner for permission when they want to borrow or need to move something that belongs to them. They take care of borrowed items and return them in good repair. A hallmark of abuse is the destruction of property valued by another.

Respect privacy. Each family member needs some personal space for privacy and solitude. Personal space gives a person a chance to develop their own uniqueness, even as they remain connected to the family. It's respectful to knock before entering someone else's space. It's respectful to provide each person in the family with a place where they can keep their belongings. One father gave each of his seven children a small lockable box in which to keep their most important treasures.

Respect other people's preferences. If your wife likes something done a certain way, think of what it would mean to her if you tried to do it that way just to please her. Respect is honoring each other's simple requests whenever possible. Tom really couldn't see why his wife had one dish towel for drying dishes and another for drying pots, but he followed her instructions anyway. She, in turn, cooked him rice the way his mother always made it, though she personally couldn't see that the result was very different from other ways of cooking it.

Respect one another's time. Ruth's dad always told her that being late was like stealing time from someone else's life. Out of respect, she decided to let others know when she was going to be late so they could plan the use of their time. It's an act of respect to express thanks for the time people generously volunteer in the interest of others.

Find ways to build people up. Marta had five young children. Josephine noticed how tired she looked as she walked down the road to buy vegetables for dinner. Wishing to give her a lift, Josephine stepped out into the street as she approached and called her over. "I've been wanting to tell you how much my son loves to come to your house and play with your children. He says you're always so kind to him. He especially likes it that you're always there to give him a drink when he's thirsty. That means a lot to me. Can't you come in for a drink and a little rest on your way to town?" Marta enjoyed her visit with Josephine and went on her way feeling better.

Mark had heard about men who respected their wives and children and treated them as if they were royalty. At first he thought it was a ridiculous idea. But he knew his home wasn't as happy it could be, so he decided to try an experiment. Without telling his family what he was doing, he planned how he would treat them like kings and queens for just one week. If things improved, he'd try it for a month. If not, he'd give up the idea. The results were amazing. By the end of the week, Mark's family were treating *him* like a king! Respect bred respect. He never looked back on his decision.

What can you do today to demonstrate the value you place on those around you? How can you make your wife feel like a ten-cow wife? What will make your children want more than anything to treat you with the respect you deserve as a return gift of love?

The Power of
One-a-Day
Multiple
Encouragements

"Therefore encourage one another and build each other up, just as in fact you are doing."—1 Thessalonians 5:11

A young mother asked her son to watch the baby for an hour while she ran an errand. The boy had an artistic bent, and as he watched his sister Sally play, he suddenly got the idea she would make a fine model. In fact, he became quite excited about drawing her picture as a surprise for his mom. Taking paper, drawing pen and ink from his art supplies, he dipped and sketched the time away, completely absorbed in his project.

By the time his mother returned, he'd nearly finished. But in his enthusiasm, he had splashed the dye all over the table, onto the rug and down his clothes. It was the kind of sight mothers dread most. As she came through the door, Ben suddenly realized what a mess he'd made. He froze, awaiting sure punishment.

But this mother took a deep breath and walked over to the table. There, to her amazement, she saw that her young son had drawn a beautiful portrait of his little sister. It was so good that she could easily see the likeness! "Why, it's Sally!" she exclaimed with delight, as she bent down and kissed him on the top of his wild curls before quietly cleaning up the mess as best she could.

Years later, this young man was called to the court of King George the Third of England as his commissioned history painter. He was Benjamin West, one of the most renowned English painters of his time. One day someone asked him what had encouraged him to become an artist. "It was a mother's kiss one day when I sketched my sister Sally's portrait!" was his immediate response. "Her encouragement did more than a rebuke ever could."

Perhaps the German writer Goethe had had a similar experience in mind when he wrote: "Correction does much, but encouragement does more."

Encouragers are very special people. Encouragers see value in others and share their enthusiasm for the goals and endeavors that give meaning to their lives. Encouragers see talent and foster its development. They are there to lift a heavy heart and offer hope in a dark moment. Encouragers care enough about you to offer a practical hand to help you reach an important goal. It doesn't matter whether the goal is a long-term one—like writing a book, getting an education, starting a new business, or being a good parent—or a short term one—such as finishing a piece of homework, cleaning up a big mess, or learning to clean a fish.

Encouragers help us stay on the road of life, even when the sun is hot, the road dusty, and the travelers tired and thirsty. They assure the weary and discouraged that the rewards will be worth the journey. A word of comfort, a sincere compliment, a listening ear and the safety of their friendship are as welcome as an oasis of rest, shade and refreshment in the desert.

Encouragement often costs the encourager nothing more than a bit of time and thoughtfulness, a few kind words, a gentle touch, a generous act. But for the person on the receiving end, a little bit of encouragement can go a long way. Remember, a kiss on the head of the young Benjamin West kept him practicing his art until he was good enough to serve the King of England. Sadly, encouragement is often in short supply. It's so easy to see the negative and to be critical of one another. It's often much harder to see the potential in a person and to focus on the positive.

Jason was busy at his desk one day when the phone rang. It was a colleague he hadn't seen for ages. "I've just called to encourage you," said Bob. "Great!" thought Jason, "I could really use some encouragement right now!" But the encouragement never came. In its place, Bob proceeded to tell Jason all the things he thought he should be doing in his job and wasn't. An hour later, when Bob was finally finished with his monologue, Jason felt more discouraged than ever. Not one word of the conversation had been encouraging.

Sarah really wanted to get along with her mother-in-law. She tried so hard to please her, but felt as if nothing she ever did was right. The children's clothes were the wrong colors, their underwear wasn't always 100% cotton, her cooking wasn't healthy enough, she didn't wash the dishes properly.

No matter how hard Sarah tried to make everything perfect, whenever her mother-in-law came by, she would always find something new to criticize. Sarah began to dread her mother-in-law's visits and started making excuses to avoid seeing her any more often than necessary. Their relationship began to crumble. Soon Sarah did all she could to avoid seeing her at all. No one likes to be around a discourager for very long.

Miss Pullen was the favorite teacher in the whole of South Lake High School. Everyone loved being in her class. She had a way of discovering something special about each of her students and encouraging them to develop their talents, whatever they were. Simon was a new student at the school. He hated writing because he'd never had any success at it. He went along to Miss Pullen's English class with a heavy heart. He was sure he'd have to write whole essays in her class, when writing even a sentence seemed overwhelming.

The first assignment was for each student to write a short piece about the things they were most looking forward to, and the things they were least looking forward to, in their new school. "That won't to be too hard," thought Simon. He would write about how much he hated writing because he never knew what words to use. Miss Pullen didn't put a grade on the assignments. Instead she wrote a personal note of encouragement to each student. She told Simon how a teacher had helped her learn to use all five of her senses when trying to describe something in writing. She also told him that personal experiences often make the best stories.

A few months later Simon had to write about his favorite place. He remembered what Miss Pullen had said. He remembered a hill where he liked to fly his kites, and he used all five of his senses to help him paint a word picture of the place. He described the songs of the birds, the humming of the kite strings, the flapping of the paper and the fabric in the breeze. He grew excited as he found words to help his teacher "see" the rainbow of color soaring in the sky, "smell" the grass as it crushed underfoot, and "feel" the wind blow through her hair. The teacher was so pleased with his work that she put it in the school magazine. Before long, English became one of Simon's favorite subjects.

Encouragement can come in all kinds of packages. Sometimes it's boxed in something as simple as a smile that brightens a child's day. Sometimes it comes wrapped in a sincere compliment like, "I like the unusual pattern in your weaving. Let's find somewhere special to display your work when you're finished!" Sometimes encouragement is an action word, lived out in simple acts of kindness like putting a chocolate on someone's desk when you know they're facing a challenge or going to the mall with a friend just because they want to be with you.

Do you know someone who needs encouragement? Is your boss under stress? Do you have a colleague who is struggling? Do you know a child who is longing to hear some encouraging words or a couple who need friends?

Emmi was working on a series of presentations for a weekend seminar. The preparation was detailed and tedious. All her spare time was focused on the project. One night she shut down her computer and rested her head on the table. "It's just too much," she cried out. "I can't do it any more. I'm so exhausted I don't care whether it's right or not."

Her husband touched her gently and said. "Don't worry, everything you do always turns out okay." As he walked away, she knew he'd wanted to encourage her, but he'd used the words that would have encouraged him! Emmi needed different words. Words like, "I know all these details seem to crowd your mind and wear you out, but I also know that the participants will really appreciate the extra touches you put into the visuals for your presentation. Let me know if I can help."

It's okay to say to someone, "I'd really like to give you a lift, but I'm not sure of the best way." Who knows? Maybe your encouragement will give someone the boost they need to create a masterpiece.

Sharing the Load

"Carry each other's burdens, and in this way you will fulfill the law of Christ."—*Galatians 6:2*

The old man struggled under the load as he carried his precious bundle of firewood down from the hills. Two young men came running along from behind. "Oh to be young again," the old man thought to himself as they came alongside him. Then, with warm smiles that dispelled his pain, the boys stopped and offered to help share the load. Leaving him the lightest portion, they shouldered the remaining sticks, and walked with him back to his home. As they went, they listened to his stories. They were stories they had heard before, but what did it matter?

Grace looked out at her garden. Tears filled her eyes as she saw the insects threatening to destroy everything she had so carefully tended. This garden was all she and her family had to depend on for sustenance. The small field suddenly looked very large as she contemplated picking off the bugs one by one. But she knew this was what she must do if there was to be anything left. Suddenly she felt a hand on her shoulder. Her husband was a man of few words. He just nodded and smiled one of his it's-going-to-be-okay smiles as he motioned for her to come with him. He had decided to put aside his own chores for the day to work with her in the garden. Grace's spirits lifted and energy returned. Together they might save something. It was a wonderful thing to know she wasn't alone, to have someone to share the load!

There's an old saying that sharing a load halves the burden. The reality may be even better than that. Gill remembers sitting on her couch paralyzed by layers of dirt on so many windows. How the picture changed when Nancy turned up at her door, bucket in hand, ready to wash windows while they chatted. Many today live life in such a rush that there seems little time or energy left for reaching out to help someone else. Many also find it difficult to accept the help, afraid somehow that this reflects negatively on their competence. It's sad when families are left to struggle in isolation when a helpful hand could make a big difference.

Kate was stricken with a rare and deadly cancer in her mid-forties. Her children were just leaving the family nest to establish lives of their own. In an unbelievable series of events in quick succession, Kate was hospitalized with life-threatening complications to her chemotherapy treatment. The family van was stolen from the parking lot outside the hospital emergency room. The owner of the home they were renting unexpectedly gave them two months notice that he would be needing the home for himself. And Kate's husband Don lost his job because his company went bankrupt in the wake of a national economic downturn. The small nuclear family was reeling with blows seemingly from every side. Thankfully, help came from every side too. Friends and extended family banded together in support. Over fifty people worked in shifts to pack up the family belongings and physically move them to another home. Many offered prayer support. Food and emergency funds appeared just when they were needed most. It seemed there was always someone sitting in the wings, offering encouragement and tending to the needs of the family in their vigil around Kate's bedside. Others searched the job listings for possibilities for Don. Still others offered help to arrange for transportation, counseling support and medical care. No one knows how they have managed, but their story is a testimony to how much the support of a caring community can mean.

Is there someone you know who is carrying a very heavy burden at the moment? Maybe they're a parent with children going through a difficult season. Maybe they have lost a loved one or experienced the heartache of death or divorce. Maybe they are without work or sufficient income for necessities. Perhaps they're new to the area or they have to care for a sick family member. Put yourself in their place and think what you'd most like someone to do for you if you were in their situation. Think about the skills, gifts, time or tangible necessities that you could offer to that person. It doesn't need to take much time to give another person some support. A little bit of care is like a few a drops of dye in a tub of water. A little goes a long way towards making today's troubles more tolerable. One of the greatest gifts we can give to another person is to anticipate their needs and find ways to meet those needs without the person having to ask. Many people find it very hard to ask for help. It's easier to accept offers.

Anne loved flowers. She and her husband Stan had always taken great pride in their beautiful garden. All her life it had given her great joy to share her flowers with those who needed a bit of love. But Stan was dead now, and Anne was stiff with age. She was finding it harder and harder to bend down to weed and clip the grass that invaded the edges. The wild look of her garden bothered her as she stared out her window, but she felt powerless to do anything about it.

One day, much to her surprise, she looked out her window and found that overnight her garden had been transformed! Friends had come quietly while she was resting and worked over her garden. They had staked the drooping flowers, trimmed back the overgrown ones, and planted some of her favorites where she could see them better from the window. Even Anne's arthritis seemed better at the sight!

There are many ways to help. We can share what we have to spare. We can give the children's outgrown clothes to a family with fast growing children. We can leave a pile of vegetables or some fresh-baked bread on the doorstep of a family where someone is sick or unable to work for a while. Even if we have very little ourselves, we can always share our time, our presence, our friendship. Running an errand, cooking a meal, mowing a lawn, taking children to the park are just a few on a starter list of things that might be done to support someone who is discouraged or in need of a lift.

Ask yourself: Is there a job my spouse hates to do or that is a real challenge for them? Can we do the job together? Could I swap jobs with someone in my family to make life easier for them? John had never been very good at math. He struggled with sorting out the family finances and paying the bills. His wife was a small woman and the big household tasks like scrubbing walls and caring for the garden were difficult for her. So they exchanged responsibilities and found that each of them managed much better.

Are your children finding their homework difficult? Do they need someone to listen to them read or to help them practice their multiplication tables? Is there perhaps a chore that they put off because it seems too big to tackle? They need to feel love in action. When we are right in there working with them, they not only *know* we love them, but they also *feel* loved.

Mitch hated cleaning out the barn. Every day after school it was his job to clean out the cattle stalls. It had to be done; he knew that. But it was back-breaking work. It was smelly, and there were always flies around. Once a month or so he'd come home from school to find the animal quarters all clean and fresh. His mom knew how much he hated the job, so she gave him a day off once in a while. When she cleaned out the stalls, Mitch felt like shouting for joy. This was a gift he could really appreciate! She did it without any comment, just as a show of support. That little bit of encouragement kept him going on all the other days when he had to do it on his own.

Jesus once went so far as to say that if someone asks you for your shirt, you should give him your coat also. If he asks you to walk a mile with him, walk for two. Human beings can be very selfish. But when one person voluntarily gives another person much more than is required, something very wonderful has happened. The person receiving the gift knows that the giver isn't giving out of a sense of duty, but out of unselfish love. For a short time at least, the giver has entered the world of another person, understood their needs and taken the time to demonstrate care in very real and tangible ways. It's a paradox, but lifting someone else's load usually makes your own feel lighter, too.

jumpstarts
for Marriage

Safe-Haven
Relationships

"I have become in his eyes like one bringing contentment."
—*Song of Songs 8:10*

Jay smiled to himself as he crawled wearily into another strange bed. It was hard being away from home. But one thing the traveling businessman could be sure about was that his wife Silla would be taking good care of everything on the home front. He smiled again as he thought about her. She was a good wife. She was intelligent, caring and always made him feel she'd choose him over a million dollars. She was his partner in marriage, in parenting, in life. They had their rough spots like all couples. But when push came to shove, he could depend on her to be right there beside him, ready to help.

Right now she was probably locking up. She'd cared for the family pets and gone through the day's mail for anything important. By now their children were sound asleep. Silla would have read them their stories, listened to their prayers, probably made a few extra trips to their bedrooms with water or to listen to some important story they had forgotten to tell her. These were simple routines, nothing very unusual or remarkable about them, but she made sure they were done tonight and every night.

Jay thought about the fact that he really should tell Silla more often how much he appreciated her reliability in the thankless routines. She had her own interests, yet for this season in their family life together, she had made the personal choice to be at home with the children. When he got back, he promised himself, he would definitely tell her how much he valued everything she did for the family. Really, that was only the beginning of what he wished he could say to Silla right now. If he were crawling into bed beside her, he would tell her how special he felt in her arms. He would tell her how much it meant to know that he could trust her. He would tell her he was a little scared about their decision to expand the business, yet how excited he was about the potential. He would hold her close and tell her how he thought about her when he was away. But the pillow talk would have to wait.

Silla hated it when Jay was away, but she knew that he needed to travel from time to time to find new customers. Even though they didn't have a lot of extras while living on one income, they always seemed to have enough. Jay had done everything in his power to make sure of that. Silla knew she was blessed. But in the busyness of the day, she didn't have a lot of time for reflection on how much the peace and security that she knew at home meant to her. Like all other moms everywhere, her day was filled with sibling squabbles, piles of washing, cooking, cleaning and repeated rounds of the same. Silla enjoyed her children, though sometimes she wondered if she were still capable of functioning in the working world or even of carrying on a conversation with anyone older than a three-year-old. She honestly couldn't remember ever having actually thanked Jay for the way he provided income for the family. She guessed she just assumed he knew she appreciated it. When he came home, maybe she'd say something. He did work long hours sometimes, and without making a big deal of it, she knew he did pay careful attention to the budget and to growing their small reserve for a "rainy day." He was a good man, and she did love him.

Silla and Jay both had a strong sense of safety and security in their relationship. This is something that is easy to take for granted when life in the family is good. Yet its importance cannot be underestimated. Drs. Archibald Hart and Sharon Morris in their excellent book *Safe-Haven Marriage*,[1] indicate that "safe-haven relationships" are one of the most significant factors contributing to a person's sense of personal peace and well-being. To be sure, Jay seldom worried about the everyday tasks of running the household. In their division of labor as a married couple, particularly now as the business was just getting started, Silla voluntarily shouldered the major responsibility for home management. Jay could trust her to do it well. Silla was able to risk a business venture because she knew Jay to be knowledgeable in business affairs, hard-working and highly committed to providing for the family's needs. But experiencing "safe haven" in a relationship is about much more than that. It is about being able to rest securely in the safety of warm, positive, lasting relationships based on strong connectedness, mutuality, care, respect, love, commitment, fidelity and the protection of lifelong covenant.

When we human beings don't feel safe and secure in family relationships, most of us experience anxiety. In such times we might not be able to express our feelings, but we feel unsettled, sometimes angry or fearful. We may experience a profound sense of sadness. The presence of these kinds of feelings often provides a good barometer reading on problems that need attention in our relationships.

Helen found it hard to feel safe in her relationship with her husband. He had always treated her very well, but when she was a child, her father had beaten her badly several times before he abandoned the family home altogether. Always in the back of her mind was the fear that Jim might also become violent towards her or abandon her suddenly with three children to rear alone.

Jim was a good husband and father. He had grown up in a safe and secure family environment. He found it hard to understand why Helen was always quizzing him about where he had been and what he was doing whenever he came home late or had to go out for the evening. She never seemed to believe him when he told her he loved her. She required a lot of reassurance about his commitment to her and the family. One day he finally asked her gently, "Don't you trust me, Helen?" Only then did Helen tell Jim the full story of her painful childhood. Jim was quick to respond. "Helen," he said, holding her close, "I want you to know that you and the children are very important to me. You are the most important people in my world, and I will always be there for all of you no matter what happens." Fortunately Helen was able to get some professional help to learn to separate her childhood pain from her relationship with Jim. All the while, Jim continued to express his love and commitment to their relationship. In time, Helen began to feel safe at last—and in turn, less suspicious, more trusting and better able to relax and enjoy their marriage and family life.

Children need to feel safe and secure in the family as well. John Bowlby, a researcher who studied the importance of warm, close bonds to a caregiver in childhood, referred to this as the fundamental human need for "attachment." Children need to know that their parents will always be there for them, whatever happens. Marci knew that her son felt safe when she was there to meet him after school. He was frightened if she were late. Because she understood this, she tried to be there a bit early each day. When she knew she would be delayed, she left a message with the school so that he would know she would be along soon.

The Klein family had a code word for the protection of their children from someone who might plan to harm them. Their code word was "peanut butter." If the parents needed to send someone to pick up the children or to give them a message, that person designated to meet the children or convey their parent's message would be told the code word. If the messenger couldn't give the code word, the children were instructed not to do as they said, but to run and tell a responsible adult right away. Without "peanut butter," the children knew the message wasn't from their parents.

Think for a few moments about what makes you feel safe in your relationships. What makes you feel unsafe? When you are afraid, what could relieve those fears and leave you feeling much more at peace? Some people may need the help of a professional counselor to find answers to these questions. Whenever there is abuse and violence in the family, safety is a big concern. It's important to ask for help from a pastor, doctor, counselor, family member or friend if you are worried about the safety of yourself and your children.

Why don't you ask your family and friends what makes them feel safe or unsafe in relationships? Then think together about what you could do to help relieve their fears. The gospel writer John observed that "Perfect loves drives out fear." Your family can learn to love in ways that inspire peace and contentment.

ENDNOTE

1 Archibald D. Hart and Sharon Hart Morris, *Safe-Haven Marriage* (Nashville, Tenn.: W Publishing Group, 2003).

Who Wants to Eat Stone Soup?

"A man who has friends must himself be friendly."
—*Proverbs 18:24 (NKJV)*

There is an old legend about a pot of soup. It seems there was to be a big meeting of village chiefs to discuss how they could work together better to share food and other resources in difficult times. Each chief was asked to bring along a vegetable to put into a pot of soup. The soup would be left to cook over the fire all day long. After the meeting, there would be plenty of soup for everyone and time to enjoy one another's company.

Chief Makuna lived in a distant village and was on the trail before sunrise. He was more than half way to the meeting when he suddenly remembered that he was supposed to bring a vegetable for the soup. He had nothing in his basket except a banana that he was planning to eat for lunch. Anyway, he couldn't put a banana in the soup. All along the path he looked for something suitable, but he didn't find anything. As he neared the village, he grew more and more concerned. He didn't want the others to know he had brought nothing to contribute. He'd have to pretend to put something into the big black pot. It would have to be something big enough to make a splash or the others would know he was faking.

Stooping down, he found a clean stone. "That'll make a nice splash!" he thought to himself. "And the stone will sink to the bottom, so it will never be served up in someone's bowl. It won't be discovered until someone cleans out the pot, and no one will ever know how it got there. Besides," he comforted himself, "everyone else will bring plenty of vegetables. There'll be more than enough. My vegetable wouldn't have made much of a difference anyway." And so it was that Chief Makuna casually dropped his stone into the boiling water and sat down proudly with the other chiefs.

The day was long and the meeting was difficult. By evening there was still much disagreement over the details of a plan for sharing resources. The chiefs were tired and looking forward to putting aside their differences over a big bowl of delicious soup. With great ceremony, the chief of the host village held up a big dipper and poured the first sampling of soup into a gourd bowl. But when he looked into the bowl, his brow wrinkled. What was this? The soup looked like nothing more than hot water! Puzzled, he stirred the big pot. Perhaps all the vegetables were on the bottom. But all he found was more hot water.

In desperation, the local chief tipped up the big black pot and poured the water onto the ground. In the bottom of the pot were eleven large stones, one for each of the other visiting chiefs. The local chief had been asked to provide the fuel for the fire instead of a vegetable, so he knew that each of the other chiefs had added only a stone to the soup pot. There was no point in filling the other bowls. There didn't seem to be much point in continuing conversations about how they would all work together for the common good of their villages either. They couldn't even cooperate to make a pot of soup!

The chiefs gained important insights that day. They had come together to make a plan for sharing resources, but they had spent all day arguing over the details. Each one of them had been more worried about making sure their village was getting its fair share than they were about helping the others. Now their hungry stomachs spoke loudly about the folly of their deliberations. Clearly each one would need to get serious about contributing something significant to the wider network if they expected the community to have adequate resources for all in a time of need.

It's not only soup that tastes better when it's rich with premium vegetables and tasty seasonings. Relationships, too, are healthier and more flavorful and satisfying the more good things we put into them. Whether village chiefs or families, neighborhoods and societies, everyone's hoping for more than "water" at the end of the day.

The good news is that we can add these wonderful ingredients at anytime we choose! Quality basic ingredients like love, mutuality, affirmation, support, commitment, loyalty, fidelity, trustworthiness and caring create the rich broth from which relationships draw their nourishment. Dashes of the herbs and spices of humor, playfulness, spontaneity and shared history give each relational pot its unique flavor.

"Stones," on the other hand, contribute nothing toward the nourishing of a relationship. Many stones actually rob soup of its flavor. They may even give it a bad taste. Some stones are really big rocks that may break the pot itself. In relationships, stones rob individuals and families of their vital energy. It takes many positive relational ingredients to override the effects of even one stone. The ratio probably needs to be at least ten relationship enhancers for every stone you let fall in the pot.

Early in a relationship, most people give a lot of attention to the ingredients they put into their soup. Building the relationship is a high priority on the agenda of all persons involved. Each one brings the best they have to the mix. But human love, by its very nature, ebbs and flows. Relationships have their seasons when they are hearty as Russian borsch served up with black bread. Most relationships, however, also have their seasons when the strength of their dynamics are more akin to the weak broth you sip when you have the flu.

Mature love is about riding out these seasons, consistently adding to the soup the best ingredients you can muster, even when you don't feel like it. Relational health is about making the choice to stir up the most tasty and nutritious creation that you can. When two people are working together to make a good relational soup, it's a good bet the result will be delicious. Even if only one spouse is adding quality ingredients and the other is still dropping stones, the flavor of the soup is likely to improve. As the aroma curling off the pot causes the taste buds of the other spouse to water, they may even begin to add better ingredients. There's nothing like anticipation to heighten experience.

Tony had started a new job and didn't get home until early evening. Finances were tight, so he had been trying to manage the home repairs and keep the car running himself. His parents weren't doing so well either, so he tried to get over there at least a couple times a week. Tammy had her job, the kids, her commitments at church. Tony was the first to realize that he and his wife had let their relational soup become a bit thin, but he didn't know where to start to restore its heartiness. He decided to try making it a point to tell his wife all the things she did that he liked. That night at dinner he reached out and touched Tammy's hand as she put a pan of cornbread down on his corner of the table. He said, "You're so busy. I can't believe you made cornbread from scratch. You know it's one of my favorites. And I like it when you wear red too," he finished with a wink. Later, when he found her humming as she booted up the computer, he leaned over her back and whispered, "Did anyone ever tell you that you brighten up this place like a canary? As a matter of fact," he went on, "you're better than any canary I could ever find."

Later that night, Tony told his wife he'd really like to know the things he did that made her happy. "I might do them more often," he said with a grin. She had to think for a while, harder and longer than he had hoped she would, but she came up with a few. "I do like it when you smile at me and when you thank me like you did at dinner. . . . It makes me happy when you tell funny stories to the children and make them laugh. . . . It's been awhile, but remember when we used to sit outside on the porch at night and look at the stars and tell each other about our dreams? I wish we could find more time for it now."

Just making a list of ingredients doesn't guarantee good soup, but it's a start. Tony and Tammy found that the more they talked about the things that made each of them feel cherished and love, the more they found themselves looking for opportunities to do them. Almost imperceptibly, their soup thickened and filled their marriage with contentment.

Bottom line—the quality of your soup is up to you! What delectable words and deeds will you drop into your soup pot today?

Open Heart
Dialogue

"Show me your face, let me hear your voice; for your voice is sweet, and your face is lovely." —Song of Songs 2:14

David sat down to supper as he had thousands of times in the forty years he and Anna had been married. Before him sat a plate of spinach lasagna. Anna smiled. She had made David this dish at least a couple of times a month since their first week of marriage.

It was her dad's favorite dish. As soon as the couple was settled, Anna lovingly set to work to prepare this very special meal. At supper-time, she watched with delight as David seemed to enjoy every bite. He saw her smiling face and told her it was the best thing he'd ever eaten. What else could he say to a brand-new wife? Little did he know that he'd have to eat that dish hundreds of times over in the next forty years. It took David forty years to pluck up the courage and find the words to let Anna know that spinach lasagna wasn't his favorite dish! Anna was surprised to learn that he preferred mushrooms to spinach in his lasagna. She had never made it that way, but she was quite willing to give it a go.

Sometimes it takes courage to communicate your thoughts and feelings, preferences and concerns, hurts and hopes. It can be especially difficult to speak of the hidden and often painful parts of your life experience. But such in-depth sharing is the key to warm, close relationships. To grow a relationship, people have to risk trusting one another enough to open themselves more and more to each other. When we trust and share, we often discover to our amazement that we are loved and accepted just the same. Such experiences are the building blocks of strong, intimate relationships.

Learning how to communicate on a deeper level is a bit like preparing yourself to compete in a high jump competition. You start off jumping over a low bar, because you know you can manage that. While practicing the low jumps, you learn how to jump safely, you learn to trust the landing mat, and gradually you improve your style. You raise the bar as you become better at jumping, but you raise it only a little at a time as you feel safe and in control. Finally you tackle the high bar, fairly confident of a sure and soft landing. But, like everyone else, you will also discover along the way that you are bound to have some not-so-good landings. You may even hurt yourself. Hopefully you can learn from these experiences and do better the next time. Just as when learning to high jump, it's best not to leap into the deepest levels of communication or into the most difficult issues right at the start of a relationship. It's better to practice on easier matters while building trust and learning the skills of dialogue.

The lowest bar on the communication high jump rack is small talk. We jump over this bar every day with comments about the weather and the social niceties we use to come and go in one another's lives. Things like, "Good morning." How was your day?" "Looks like rain." "It's nice to meet you." "Have a good evening."

The next higher bar is factual information. People negotiate this level successfully when they pass on snippets of news and exchange the particulars necessary for smooth family functioning. Dialogue at this level is filled with things like the fact that Billy has a big math test tomorrow and would like to study in the family room tonight with some of his classmates, or the observation that the garden needs watering, or the fact that Tom and his friends are going on a camping trip and want to use the family tent. In families that are not functioning well, information is often withheld by family members as a means of control. Families cannot live together in harmony without information.

Raising the bar to the third level, you offer your opinion about things. Around the family circle you hear comments like, "I think the new chemistry teacher is going to work out well. She seems to be willing to take the time to really explain things." "I think it's good for Billy and his friends to study together. They can all help each other when they get stuck on a problem."

The fourth level adds feelings to the communication mix. "Our old chemistry teacher used to make us feel so stupid. I like our new teacher because she can even make you feel smart for asking a good question!" "I'm feeling pretty good about the "B" I got on my math test. It was a hard test over some pretty difficult concepts, but my study paid off." "You must feel proud of yourself, Billy. You've improved your grades in both math and English this year."

The highest level of communication involves sharing your innermost self—your secrets, your hopes for the future, your fears, your dreams, your discouragements. "I have always dreamed of working in a chemistry lab. Our new teacher is starting to convince me I could be good at it." "I hate math!. I have never forgotten the time I got a sum wrong and the teacher humiliated me in front of the whole class. Right now, I can't get my check book reconciled with my bank statement. Do you think you could help me with it over the weekend?"

In families where there is an atmosphere of acceptance, love and trust, open communication can have amazing results. Samuel was worried about money. He was working hard, but there were so many bills. He never talked to his wife about money, because when he got married he was advised by other men that it was never a good idea to let your wife know how much you earned. "She'll just want to spend it all!" they said.

At a family seminar, Samuel and his wife Elizabeth heard the leader couple dialogue about their family finances. Samuel was quite amazed at the good suggestions the wife offered, but he thought about this experience for a long while before he decided to talk about his finances with Elizabeth. He told her that he was worried about their growing debts and eventually disclosed exactly how much he earned. Together they agreed on a budget and committed themselves to the changes necessary to improve their financial state.

When Samuel related this story later, he had a wide grin on his face. It seems that after talking with his wife, she didn't go out and spend all his money after all. Rather, once Elizabeth understood their circumstances, she worked harder to stretch every dollar. She even took in sewing to increase their income. Samuel hadn't become rich, but he was definitely pleased! Elizabeth enjoyed the rewards of her husband's affirmation and trust and was excited about her new sewing business. She said their relationship had never been stronger.

One of the biggest barriers to good communication is fear. When a person is afraid that what they say might be misunderstood or taken the wrong way, they often don't bother saying anything. But communication isn't optional. It is a key building block for strong relationships. A good place to start is by communicating openly yourself. Share a goal you would really like to achieve or something you wish you could enjoy together. Then invite your spouse or friend to share their hopes and aspirations. Talk together about how you might help one another make these hopes and desires a reality.

Listening well is one of the best ways of encouraging good communication. Listen without being critical or defensive. Sum up occasionally with comments that reflect the thoughts and feelings shared. "So you're saying I could help you by...." or "You're really feeling ... about your boss's reaction to your idea." This kind of conversation develops skills that can help you deal with more difficult issues later.

Children are drawn to good listeners. Take time to give them undivided attention and show you're interested in what they have to say. Some families plan for a few minutes of sharing time around the dinner table at night, giving each person a chance to share the best thing and the worst thing that happened to them that day. When your children want to talk to you, look at them. Touch them as they feel comfortable, and don't try to read a newspaper at the same time! Go for a walk or out for a treat. Take them to a quiet place where you won't be distracted by other things. Older children may talk more freely when they feel relaxed and able to escape when they don't want to talk more—like when you're washing the car or playing a game.

Is there someone longing to be closer to you today? Share your dreams with them and listen to theirs. It could be the beginning of something wonderful!

Nurturing Love's
Tender Shoots

"Put . . . religion into practice by caring for [your] own family, . . . for this is pleasing to God." —*1 Timothy 5:4*

atyana stared blankly from her cot. Her mother and father had both been killed in a raid on their village before she could walk or talk. Now three years old, she seldom left her bed. Some kind people provided resources for her basic necessities, but she had never known what it meant to be loved. She had never learned to play or speak.

Knowing that we are loved and cared for is a very important part of our physical and emotional development. We can give children all the basic necessities, but if they don't feel loved, something very important inside of them will wither and die. Adults aren't much different. Everyone needs to know someone cares. To have a healthy, growing marriage, both partners need to know that they are cherished. Happily for Tatyana, a caring family adopted her and loved her as their own. Slowly, over several years, love worked its miracle. The silent, withdrawn little girl has learned to trust, talk, smile, play and to love in return.

Mary and her husband were living parallel lives. Now it seemed they shared nothing except their three daughters. The relationship was convenient, but the warm feelings present when they were married had died. Mary decided to seek advice from an older woman. "Feelings often follow action when it comes to loving," the wise woman said knowingly. "If you want to love Carl again, begin by doing something loving for him every day."

It sounded much too simple to Mary, and her heart wasn't really in it. But she had asked for advice, and she felt duty-bound to give it a try. The first day she slipped his favorite snack into his lunch-box. The next week, she found a recording—one that Carl had been talking of buying for a long time. It wasn't her taste in music, but she knew he liked it, so what could she lose? After that, she mended his comfy old sweater that he'd ripped in the garden. Soon it became almost a hobby trying to find caring things to do for him. She certainly hadn't expected to enjoy it this much. She clearly remembers the day she felt a tiny little thrill inside her when Carl gave evidence that he had noticed something special she had done for him. Slowly positive feelings toward one another were reborn, and the love they thought was dead once again showed signs of life.

Loving care isn't always easy. There are lots of niggling little things that damage a relationship, just like little caterpillars nibbling away and destroying a beautiful plant. Often the biggest barriers to tender loving care are unresolved hurts transformed into resentment and anger. Kim had planned a special evening for her husband Tom. He'd been working hard all week, and they'd barely seen each other. She was at home caring for three small children, and there wasn't much money for luxuries. She thought it would be fun to have a special evening at home together.

Kim planned for everything! Tom's favorite meal, a lovely table set with flowers and candles, children in bed early. She put on her best dress and anxiously anticipated Tom's arrival. The usual time of his arrival home passed. A half hour, then an hour went by. But still he didn't come. She waited and waited, keeping the food warm as best she could. After awhile she began to feel angry, resentful and hurt. "He didn't even have the decency to call," she muttered to herself. Now her dinner was ruined! With a huff, she blew out the candle stubs and headed for bed.

But she couldn't sleep. She could only lie there fuming. Where was Tom anyway? How dare he stay out late without calling. Why didn't he think about her for a change? Now all her efforts were for nothing. When he came in, she decided, she was really going to give him a piece of her mind, and a big piece, too!

Suddenly the train of her thoughts shifted unexplainably. But I love Tom! This is not like him. I do hope he's safe! He's more important to me than anyone else in the world. Right now he is probably wishing more than anything that he was at home. He must be so tired and discouraged from having to sort out so many problems at work. The last thing he needs is to come home to an angry wife!

As she thought about Tom's needs, her heart softened. Instead of feeling angry, hurt and resentful, her heart filled with love and care for Tom. By the time he came home, Kim was a different person. She had brought down his slippers, pulled together the pieces of the newspaper, and prepared to reheat his supper. She found some fresh candles and sat down with him while he ate. She listened as he told her how much he'd wanted to get home, but he'd been helping a family through a crisis.

"You know, Kim," he said, "I'm so sorry I wasn't able to call you and let you know where I was, but there was no phone there. I was expecting you to be really mad at me for coming home so late. All day long I had to deal with angry and upset people. It's so good to come home and feel loved and cared for by you. You don't know how much I appreciate that." Kim's resentment could easily have ruined the evening and maybe even done lasting damage to the relationship. Fortunately, somewhere along the way, Kim had learned something very important about true love.

Is there something that gets in the way of your close relationships? Is there something that stops you from showing love and care to those around you? Maybe it's just that you are too tired to be bothered any more. Or perhaps it's just too much effort to think about anyone else's needs except your own. Can you simplify your life a little, or ask for some extra help, or find more time to sleep?

Maybe you have been hurt badly in a relationship and loving feelings are at a low ebb. In order to preserve the safety and well-being of yourself and your children, it may be necessary to bring a destructive relationship to an end. You owe it to yourself and others who are vulnerable to seek professional counsel to weigh the alternatives open to you and to determine whether or not it is safe to consider giving this relationship a second chance.

Do you need ideas for showing tender loving care? Try these for starters. A little note of appreciation tucked into a pair of socks or a book bag. A special card or e-mail that puts your loving thoughts and feelings into words. Your undivided attention when someone you love is talking. A gentle, loving touch with no sexual overtones. A small gift you know will bring delight. A sincere thank you. A tidy-up of the house. Doing someone else's chores without being asked, especially a chore you know they really dislike.

People are different, so it's really important to discover what makes people feel loved and cared for. Paul liked having his back rubbed, so he assumed that Bonnie would like having hers rubbed too. But backrubs made Bonnie feel even more uptight. She preferred for Paul to make her a hot cup of herbal tea and serve it in her prettiest tea cup and saucer. She laughed the evening he served her tea with a towel over his arm!

Kandy once asked her children what made them feel special. She was expecting to hear something big or costly, but they said simple things like "when you cook macaroni," "when you help me with my homework," or "when you smile at me when I'm singing in the choir."

Steve knew his wife liked flowers, but it was difficult for him to spend his hard-earned money on fresh ones that would soon wither. So he came up with what seemed to him a very practical solution. He would buy flowers in pots so they would last longer. Unfortunately, his wife Nita did not have a green thumb. The potted plants inevitably died, and she felt terribly guilty. Fortunately, Steve and Nita were able to talk about what was happening. She gave him a list of all the plants she'd like to have in the garden where they'd need less attention. That way Steve could be sure that the flowers would be enjoyed as the gifts of love he intended them to be.

Loving care is a vital ingredient in healthy relationships. It has potent, restorative powers even in hurting relationships. You can start today by reaching out to someone close to you and surprising them with a gesture of love.

Celebrating
Differences

"We have different gifts, according to the grace given us."
—Romans 12:6

Naomi was quiet and self-assured. She liked people, but she was also very content to be alone. She had many projects that interested her and especially enjoyed reading and working in her garden. She loved bright colors and spilled their cheer into her wardrobe, her furnishings, and her landscaping. She was creative and generous, but she liked to plan ahead and go about life in an organized fashion.

Her friend Nathan loved the outdoors, taking every opportunity to participate in sports like hiking and rock climbing. Around people, Nathan was witty and talkative, always part of making any gathering a good time for everyone. Nathan's friends joked about the "Nathan uniform," because he always wore kaki's and a dark t-shirt. "It doesn't show the dirt," Nathan would retort with a laugh. While, on the one hand, he was an active, spontaneous, easy-going kind of guy, when it came to money, he was very careful with his spending and kept meticulous accounts.

As their friendship blossomed into marriage, Nathan and Naomi were drawn to each other by their differences. Naomi found that Nathan's peaceful and calm manner made him feel rested and refreshed. She liked listening to him talk. He found that he quite liked her bright colors and enjoyed the neighbors' compliments about her landscaping. She got better at shopping for bargains, and he experienced new joys in giving.

But, after a while, these differences began to look less attractive. Nathan wished that Naomi would be just a little more outgoing. Naomi wished Nathan wouldn't go out so much without her. She wanted to stay home more often, but with him! And she wished he would expand his wardrobe. Kaki's and dark tees were okay, but she felt hurt that he never wore the brightly-dyed shirts she bought for him. Nathan began to suggest aloud that the upholstery fabrics Naomi had chosen for the house might be a bit loud. She got tired of always having to shop for the cheapest price on everything. He thought she was careless with money. Nathan wanted Naomi to loosen up and be more spontaneous. She thought that his last minute planning created altogether too much stress and chaos.

So, Naomi and Nathan began to argue. Soon they found many things to be irritated about. The atmosphere at home was often tense and miserable. Sometimes they didn't speak to each other for hours, maybe even into the next day. What had gone wrong? Both were highly committed to the marriage. Would they have to live with this frustration all of their lives?

In reality, the choice is theirs. What has happened to Naomi and Nathan is a pretty typical scenario for many couples. A well-known marriage and family therapist, Carl Whitaker, suggests that it's not that couples have differences, but the way a couple deals with differences that will determine the quality of their relationship. He identifies a step-by-step process for dealing with differences that can actually lead to a celebration of differentness rather than to the kinds of frustration and growing resentment that threaten Naomi and Nathan's marriage.

The first step in dealing with differences in a more effective way is to *acknowledge* that the differences exist. Early in relationships, couples tend to be in denial about their differentness. Each wants to see the other as close to perfect, and both are willing to accommodate almost any behavior in order to keep the dream of an idyllic marriage alive. But as the friction created by the differences builds, denial becomes impossible to maintain. At this point many partners put forth an all-out effort to change one another. However, it is an effort predictably doomed to failure and further frustration.

According to Whitaker, if the couple is to grow toward intimacy, denial must give way to *acceptance*. It is important to be clear here that we are talking about acceptance of the usual kinds of differences that couples know. We are not talking about acceptance of abusive or violent behavior. Abuse and violence are terribly destructive of persons and relationships. It is often unsafe for such relationships to continue, and such behavior never leads to a strong, healthy marriage. But for "garden variety" differences, acceptance is a necessary next step. Acceptance opens the way for Naomi to accept Nathan as more outgoing and spontaneous, as preferring neutral colors and familiarity in clothing, etc., without passing judgment on him as a person for having these preferences. Acceptance helps her view Nathan as "different," but not necessarily "wrong."

At Whitaker's third stage of growth toward handling differences effectively, the couple come to *respect* each other with their differences. As respect develops between them, Nathan begins to see the ways in which Naomi's differentness complements his own. He finds himself admitting on occasion that it's a good thing Naomi is not exactly like he is. If she were, they'd never stay home and get chores done around the house. And he would miss the "color" she brings into his life. Naomi knows her husband's careful financial management has made it possible for them to buy a home, and he appreciates her skill and effort in making their home an welcoming place to which to return at the end of a long day.

Many couples know the satisfaction of coming to actually *enjoy* their partner, differences and all! At this new plateau of learning to deal with differences well, Naomi finds herself shaking her head with a smile as she picks up Nathan's soccer ball so she can get the garage door closed. She never would have been to a soccer game if she hadn't married Nathan. Come to think of it, there are many things she probably never would have tried or experienced if she had not linked her life with his. Meanwhile Nathan has to admit how special his wife really is as he comes home to a candlelight table set for two. He has come to appreciate the deep level of dialogue and the feelings of closeness that such romantic evenings provide. Sometime along the way, if Naomi and Nathan continue to grow together, they will awake to the realization that they have truly come to *treasure* one another and to cherish one another just as they are.

So how can you begin this journey and find your way to such a satisfying end-of-the road? Firstly, try thinking back to a time when you both had positive attitudes toward each other. Think about the qualities in each other that you used to appreciate. Write them down and spend some time contemplating each quality and what it has meant to you. How has it enriched your life or contributed to your happiness? What would it be like to live without that quality in your partner? It may help to remember that you have your own characteristics that others may find irritating! If you treat others with tolerance and good humor, they're much more likely to treat you the same way. When you're irritated by a characteristic in your spouse, think about how the different skills and qualities possessed by the other person have the potential to make your relationship stronger. Ask yourself, "What have we been able to accomplish together that neither of us could have accomplished alone?" Anticipate how you might combine your gifts for future good.

One husband, on seeing the results of personality testing done by a counselor during the early years of marriage, blurted out, "This marriage may well self-destruct!" The test highlighted many differences, and as predicted, learning to deal with these differences constructively had not been easy. But now, approaching forty years of marriage, the couple shared this moment of celebration:

Recently they visited a beautiful national park. It was early Spring, and nature was alive with flowers, bird songs and animals with young. Jill would have been content to sit in the first meadow for the entire two days they had to spend in the park, identifying flowers and birds and delighted by the occasional visit of a family of deer or prairie dogs. Jim would have tackled the park, map in hand, carefully charting his course to take in as much terrain as possible. At the entrance to the park, the two stopped at a welcome center with a small gift shop. Coming together again at the door a few minutes later, both had something behind their backs. Jill brought her arm around from behind her to reveal a map she had bought with Jim in mind. Jim had purchased a book identifying birds and flowers resident in the park. They had so come to treasure one another, differences and all, that their greatest joy was in offering their beloved two days in the park as they would enjoy it most. It can happen for you too, if you choose to take the journey together.

One of the Ten

"But God demonstrates his own love for us in this: While we were still sinners, Christ died for us." —*Romans 5:8*

Grandma Ethel and Grandpa Joe had celebrated their 55th wedding anniversary. Grand-daughter Amy, just engaged to be married, was sitting with Grandma Ethel watching Grandpa Joe work in the vegetable garden.

"Fifty-five years is a long time, Grandma," admired Amy. "How ever have you managed to stay happily married for so long?"

"Well, it wasn't always easy. When I first married Grandpa Joe, he did all kinds of things I didn't much like. I'd think to myself, "How will I ever manage being married to a man like that for a lifetime!" One day I wrote down the things I didn't like about him or that I didn't like him doing. I stopped with a list of about ten."

"Only ten?" smiled Amy.

"Well, maybe a few more than that! Anyway, I knew I wouldn't leave him for these kinds of things, and I knew I couldn't change him. So what did I do? I decided that instead of getting all frustrated and irritated by Joe's "little ways," I'd see them as something special about him that made him Joe, the man I loved and married."

"How did you manage to do that?"

"Well, every time he did something on my list—like slurp his spaghetti or forget to take off his muddy boots outside—I'd think to myself, "I'll give that to him as a gift.""

"You mean you never tried to change him or tell him you didn't like what he did?"

"Oh no, I'm not that perfect! Sometimes I'd forget all about my list, and sometimes something I thought I could accept really started to cause bad feelings. Then I'd have to talk to your grandfather about it. But there were many little things I decided not to get irritated about and just let them go."

"But what if Grandpa behaved really badly? You wouldn't have said anything to him?" Amy was horrified.

"Of course I would have. I'm not talking here about really hurtful behavior. I'm talking about the kinds of differences couples have to learn to deal with. I guess I must have my funny little ways too, and they must drive him half-crazy! But maybe because I accept him, crazy little ways and all, he has been able to accept me too.

"I've seen some couples nearly destroy their relationship over the little things. He walks in with his muddy shoes, and she gets angry at him. He feels humiliated and cross inside, so when she burns the rice, or irons a crease in his shirt, it's like he's looking for a reason to get back at her. And so anger escalates."

"So what were those ten annoying things that Grandpa Joe did?" Amy was curious.

"Believe it or not, I have the hardest time remembering! So now, if he does something not to my liking, my first thought is that whatever he has done this time must have been on that list. I say to myself, "It's just one of the ten." So I let it go. Often the things that annoy us most are the little things that don't matter very much in the long run. I ask myself, "Next week, will it really matter that Joe spilled soup on his best shirt or brought some mud into the kitchen?" Then I decide once more that it is more important to show him love and acceptance than to worry about a few laundry stains and a little mud."

"So that's how you've been so happy all these years?"

"Yes, Amy. It might sound too simple to some people, but it's worked for your grandfather and me. I never have felt he took advantage of my attitude either. I actually think he loves me for it." Grandma Ethel has learned the secret of acceptance. She has learned to look beyond the differences and human foibles to see Grandpa Joe's true worth shining underneath. And it has made all the difference in the quality and durability of Joe and Ethel's marriage.

Margaret went to the store with her son Pete. He had his head shaved except for a long strip down the middle that was tied back into a ponytail. He had rings in his nose and five studs in his left ear. He had a tattoo all down one arm and a black leather jacket held together by large metal safety pins. After they had paid for their goods, Pete loaded his arms with his mom's bags and headed for the door. "Aren't you embarrassed to be seen with him?" asked the girl at the counter when Pete was out of ear shot.

"Oh, no!" replied Margaret. "He's my son! Looks don't tell everything, you know. Not many sons would give up an afternoon to take their mother shopping."

It's easy to look at others and find something to criticize. It's easy to find reasons to exclude them from the group or to make them feel they can never do anything right. But rejection hurts, and it hurts even more when it comes from your own family.

Joanna was hurting. She was the youngest of four sisters. All her life she knew her father wished she were a boy. He called her Jo, bought her a football and took her fishing. Joanna didn't mind football or fishing or being called Jo, but she felt her dad's acceptance only when she was doing what he considered to be "boy-things." He didn't like seeing her in dresses. And he wouldn't let her grow her hair long. She grew up and went to law school, always trying to please him. Even after experiencing considerable success in her profession, she still wasn't happy. She was doing it all for her dad. She longed for his unconditional acceptance, but it never came. It seemed her efforts would always be short of his expectations.

Non-acceptance is one of the quickest ways to set up barriers between people. Rejection is a way of putting oneself above another person. We dare to think that we are better than others, forgetting we're also imperfect and often make mistakes as well. Acceptance frees us to accept others and to be comfortable with ourselves, even though no one is perfect.

Dr. Lawrence stood in the corner of the hospital room. There were tears in his eyes. He'd just told Arianne, a beautiful girl in her mid-twenties, that she would never smile properly again. She had been in a serious accident, and her face had been badly cut. The wounds were healing well, but the cut had been so deep that her mouth would always be twisted. As the surgeon updated her medical chart beside her hospital bed, her young husband Scott arrived for a visit. Arianne was obviously concerned about his reaction. Would he still love her, looking like some distorted clown? She smiled a shaky smile as he walked towards her. He looked at her. A flicker of surprise was reflected in his eyes. "Sorry about my face," she murmured. "I wouldn't blame you if . . ."

As the doctor watched in silence, Scott stopped her in mid-sentence. "Something about you looks prettier than ever!" was all that the young husband said. Then he took her face in his hands and bent down to kiss her. Dr. Lawrence was amazed as he saw the young husband twist his own mouth as he kissed hers, carefully matching their lips and making sure she knew their kiss still worked. From that moment on the doctor had no fears about Arianne's ability to cope with her disfigurement.

That moment marked the beginning of Arianne's full recovery. In time she would be able to accept herself, in large part because Scott accepted her. Without his acceptance, she may have hidden herself away from life, embarrassed to be seen. But with his acceptance, she eventually had the courage to go anywhere she wanted, to meet new people and to smile her own unique smile. She found a new freedom in knowing that people valued her for who she really was and not just because she was beautiful.

Is there someone in your life who needs to feel your acceptance? Is there someone struggling with rejection, longing to hear a positive word from you? Is there someone wishing you'd invite them to your home or out to lunch, someone who longs to see your smile? Just as much as we long to be accepted by others, many also long to be accepted by us. It's wonderful when we find someone who will accept us without demanding changes in the ways that make us unique persons. In such a relationship, we are freed to be ourselves and to grow toward the kind of person we really want to be. And the more accepting we are of others, the more likely they will be to accept us and overlook all those little things we do that can be irritating. Grandma Ethel and Grandpa Joe were onto something big!

Sexuality 101 for the
Experienced and
Inexperienced

"There are three things that are too amazing for me, four that I do not understand: the way of an eagle in the sky, the way of a snake on a rock, the way of a ship on the high seas, and the way of a man with a maiden." —Proverbs 30:18, 19

Sex gets a lot of press. It sells books, movies, talk shows, toothpaste, reality TV, and even the news. At the same time, myth and ignorance abound. Parents struggle for words, and many couples report low levels of sexual satisfaction in their marriages. What would you put in the syllabus for Sexuality 101 if it were required coursework for this generation?

Sexuality is a big word. It is at the core of who we are as human beings. Sexuality begins with feeling good about being male or female. A sense of gender well-being is developed from birth when parents celebrate the birth of both sons and daughters and provide warmth and affection irrespective of gender. It grows as all parts of the body and their functions are affirmed as good. Something as simple as teaching a child the proper name for their penis or vagina helps to create the overall sense that sexuality is a good gift. Children who emerge from childhood with good feelings about their bodies and accurate information about sexuality appropriate to their age level are far ahead of children left to pick up their facts on their own.

Researchers studying more than 150 societies worldwide have concluded that human beings everywhere fall in love and that the relationship between a man and a woman develops in at least two stages: attraction and attachment. One anthropologist who observed the human bonding process, found that with minor cultural variation, a predictable sequence of steps could be identified between the first look of attraction and the intimate experience of sexual intercourse.[1] A sequence of relational tasks emerges from a study of Morris' work that are vital to safe and satisfying sexual intimacy in marriage. These tasks take the couple from attraction, to discovery of one another as persons, through an evaluation and affirmation of this person as a potential life partner, to a decision to pursue the relationship at deeper levels. The relationship must then deepen through self-disclosure and the building of mutual respect, care, trust and acceptance. It culminates with the promise of lifelong commitment in marriage and the full giving of each to the other in sexual intimacy.

In his book *Bonding: Relationships in the Image of God,* Donald Joy highlights several other important findings that grow out of this research.[2] The best bonds are found among couples whose relationships develop slowly, who complete the relational tasks associated with deepening levels of intimacy, and whose mature love coincides with marriage and their ability to take up adult responsibilities. It has been recognized that with the commencement of self-disclosure, the relationship intensifies considerably. When relationships break up after couples have shared deeply emotionally or engaged in sexual intimacies, significant pain will likely result. Promiscuous sexual behavior has also been shown to put at risk a person's capacity to permanently bond.

For marrieds, an understanding of the processes of attraction and attachment can help spouses to strengthen their relationships by regularly renewing their early attentions to one another and continuing to grow in their love and commitment within marriage. Such intentionality in the protection of their marriage bonds is the best antidote to illicit relationships and divorce.

Beth knew that her husband Joe was special. He wasn't perfect, but he was kind, gentle and willing to carry his share of home responsibilities. He found many ways to show how much he respected and cherished her. For her, sex was a gift of herself to him which grew naturally out of the love they shared. Joe knew he had been fortunate. His parents had a good marriage. Their affection for one another was a large piece of the security he had known as a child. As Joe had been able to understand, both his parents had been very open with their son about sexuality. Here are some highlights from Joe's "course" in Sexuality 101.

For Joe's folks, there was no one else. Both poured all their sexual energies into their marriage relationship. Joe remembers his dad telling him one time that though he had always been faithful to his marriage vows, he had reached a point when he found himself pouring more and more into the marriage. "It's like I turned a corner one day from which I knew I would never turn back. It was your mom, and your mom alone, for me."

Joe's dad could appreciate the book title he saw in a bookstore once, *Sex Begins in the Kitchen*. He understood it was no good expecting his wife to be interested in sex for one hour in a day if during the other 23 hours their relationship had been filled with silence, disrespect and unresolved anger and conflict. It was the attention, support, respect, care and love that he showed throughout the day that formed the bedrock for their sexual play.

Joe also learned from his parents that good sex is about giving and receiving, never about force. It's about being considerate when your partner is stressed or emotionally and physically overdrawn. It means being willing to put your own needs and desires on hold from time to time in the interest of your partner's needs. It means recognizing that sometimes your partner may desire soothing touch that does not lead to sexual intercourse. Joe's dad knew the meaning of the maxim, "Sex is never an emergency." He had chuckled when he told Joe, "Look, when your wife just isn't able tonight, remember no man ever died because he couldn't have sex when he wanted it." A good sexual relationship requires a mutuality that takes into consideration the comfort zone of each partner and a willingness on the part of both to confine their sexual practices to those that both of them find pleasurable.

Joe's parents talked to him about the differences between men and women in their sexual response. "Men," Joe's dad told him, "typically want sex more often and are quickly aroused by visual stimuli. Women, on the other hand, are usually more slowly aroused and appreciate pillow talk and long periods of gentle caress of the full body as well as the breasts and genitals." It was from his parents that Joe learned about the clitoris, the female organ located just above the vaginal opening and the urethra, whose only purpose is pleasure and arousal for women. Joe came to his wife Beth knowing the value of gentle touch, time and tenderness in bringing his wife to full arousal.

One thing Joe and Beth were careful to guard was their personal, private circle of love. They had many friends and, from time to time, participated in a marriage strengthening program offered in their community. But they had an understanding between them that their sexual love was their own beautiful experience, and that neither of them would talk about it with friends. Instead, they learned to talk with each other. They understood that a good sexual relationship is not about perfect technique, nor about performance. Over time they became more and more open in their dialogue, guiding and teaching one another in the ways of lovemaking both enjoyed most.

Fortunately for Joe and Beth, their expectations were realistic. They had been coached by the generation before them to expect the inevitable ebb and flow of human love. They knew there would be moments of ecstasy as well as other moments when weariness, stress and the humdrum of life would drain away their desire. They anticipated the seasons when changes like new babies, moving and career shifts would make it necessary for them to be more intentional about attending to the sexual needs of one another.

Joe and Beth also came to the realization in a marriage enrichment program they attended that most all couples experience trouble of one sort or another at some time, and that trouble in the relationship will almost surely be reflected in sexual satisfaction. They liked the illustration the presenter used of an overloaded banana truck stalled out at the crest of an incline on a narrow mountain road. As traffic backed up behind the laboring truck, the drivers finally got out and together pushed the struggling vehicle over the top. "Marriage can be like that," the presenter said. "The good news is, when you need help, there are usually people around who can give you a push. And if you need a big push, ask someone you trust to help you find someone who has the professional skills to get you back on the road toward where you want to go."

Think what could happen if such a Sexuality 101 were available in every family!

ENDNOTE

1   Desmond Morris, *Intimate Behaviour* (New York: Random House, 1971).

2   Donald Joy, *Bonding: Relationships in the Image of God* (Nappanee, Ind.: Evangel Publishing House, 1986).

New Beginnings

"Be completely humble and gentle; be patient, bearing with one another in love." —*Ephesians 4:2*

Don and Liz were good friends with Molly and Malcolm. As neighbors, they often picked up the mail, pulled a package in out of the rain, or mowed the lawn in the other's absence. There had really never been any trouble between them, until their two college-aged kids eloped over spring break. Never had Liz felt more devastated in all her life than she did when she got the news. The call from their daughter and new son-in-law had ended with Liz sobbing uncontrollably and Don talking for both of them: "I just don't know how you could do this to your mother! You know she has looked forward to planning your wedding since the day you were born! I can't believe this is happening to us. . . ." Molly and Malcolm got the news too and wanted to come over to talk, but Liz was in no mood to talk to anyone. Don made excuses, said they'd talk later, but now a week had gone by and there had been no contact.

When Marlene's mom died, her will made provision for her estate to be divided equally among her four children. The document had not, however, been specific as to the distribution of her household and personal effects. Marlene made the day's drive to help her brothers to pack things up and prepare the house for sale. Arriving ahead of them, Marlene unlocked the door and stepped inside. The second she walked into the vestibule, she noticed some of her mom's most treasured possessions were already gone. The mantel clock that had chimed in the living room since her childhood was not in its usual place. The largest pieces from her mom's collection of treasured figurines had been removed from the display case. A quick trip through the house revealed that the good silver and great-grandma's tea set were also gone. Marlene felt her muscles tighten and her heart begin to race. What gave her brothers and their wives the right to just help themselves with no consideration of her desires whatsoever? Impulsively, Marlene turned on her heel, locked the house and headed for home.

In the movie *The Story of Us*, Katie and her husband Ben are past brushing aside the twinges of irritation. They've grown tired of forcing smiles in public when inside they both know they are not the "happy couple" everyone thinks they are. In his opening soliloquy, Ben says that when they were first married, he expected their marriage would be like the stories he'd heard of old married couples. Couples who, after 50 or 60 years of living together, were so close and loving that when one of them died, the other died too, of a broken heart. Katie had loved Ben for his creative, spontaneous, free spirit. It awakened the uninhibited part of her and broke the yoke of work and schedules that smothered the fun girl inside. But the dream of living "happily ever after" had been shattered by disillusionment.

"You never listen," Katie screams in desperation.

"You can't let go of anything!" Ben retorts.

Katie comes back hard: "So I haven't done anything right for 15 years?"

Ben is now on the attack. "Well, why does everything have to be programmed? Can't you ever do anything spontaneous? What happened to the fun girl I married?"

"She died, and you killed her!" Katie fires back in an argument-clinching rebound.

As the movie reaches its climax, Ben and Katie have decided to put an end to their marriage. They will take the kids home and begin by telling them what wonderful kids they are and how much they love them. Then they will simply tell them that Mommy and Daddy love each other too, but in a different way now, and that's why they are getting a divorce. There seems no way to recover happier times.

There's probably not a person alive who hasn't wished more than once that they could just turn back the clock. "If only . . ." is a common refrain in the self-talk of most of us. What do you do when you find yourself mired down in circumstances, often at least partly of your own making, and wishing like everything you could back up and begin again?

Give yourself some time and space. Relational crises leave you spinning. Adrenaline runs high and inhibits clear thinking. It's hard to get perspective. Often the best gift you can give yourself and others involved is a chance to recover your composure and your heart rate. Say things like, "I really want to be part of resolving this situation with you, but I need some time to think about what I would really like to say and do." Some people prefer time alone. Others need to talk with someone whom they trust and who has enough emotional distance from the situation to be able to listen and help the person involved to clarify their thinking and weigh the alternatives open to them.

Think long-range. When emotions are running high, it's hard to think beyond the trauma of the moment. It's much easier to be reactive than proactive, to do what feels good now rather than considering the likely effects of various courses of action over time. Ask yourself questions like, "What do I really wish could happen in this situation?" "What could I say and do which would increase the likelihood that this problem would be resolved with relationships intact?" "What kinds of words and actions on my part might threaten this relationship in the long term?"

Try reframing the faces. In the heat and hurt of the moment, a person's vision easily takes on the properties of a high resolution magnifying glass that enlarges the faults and foibles of others. Take the time to think of each person involved in the difficult situation you are facing, one by one. Try to see the situation from their vantage point. Think about the difficulties they have encountered in life that have brought them to this point. Try to frame each face with an understanding of the person's humanness and limitations.

Consider becoming a transitional person. Every person alive comes to relationships with a history. We all carry baggage from the past. Each person brings to a relationship their own "suitcase" of preferences, life experiences, hopes and dreams. Some bags contain hazardous materials that can put close relationships at risk. Some suitcases are filled with such relational toxins to overflowing. Are there destructive patterns in your family relationships that need to be changed if the family is to be healthy? Contemplate what it would be like if you were to make a decision to clean up what you could of the poisonous waste in your suitcase and choose not to pass this heritage on to the next generation. You aren't likely to be able to change another person. But what changes can you make in yourself and in your ways of relating that might set your family on a course that leads to new life?

Check your sheet inventory. An old radio preacher brought to life the story of a teenager in conflict with his parents. In typical fashion, both the teen and the parents said things in the heat of conflict that drove them into opposite corners. Things were said along the way that were hard to take back. Finally, the teenager left home for the big city, and for years there was only occasional contact. In the meantime, the parents mellowed and the teen grew up.

One day a letter arrived. "I know I have hurt you deeply, but I would like to come home," was all the explanation it offered. "I'll be coming through on the 7:05 train. If you want to see me, hang a white handkerchief from the back fence. I'll see it when the train rounds the bend. If not, I'll understand. Your son." The parents were overwhelmed with emotion. This was the day they had longed for, yet their hearts were still tender. He could hurt them again.

But the risk didn't deter them long. Springing into action, the old couple opened drawers and cupboards from attic to laundry room, pulling out sheets, towels, handkerchiefs, everything white they could find. They hung them from the fence, the clothesline, even the trees. A dramatic message in white: "Come home, dear son, come home!"

Katie's closing monologue in the movie The *Story of Us* moves the couple from despair to new beginnings. "We are an *us*," she explains. "There's history here, and histories don't happen overnight.....It's a dance you perfect over time. And it's hard, much harder than I thought it would be. But there's more good than bad, and you don't just give up!" If yours is a relationship worth saving, perhaps you can find it in yourself to hang out a white-sheet invitation to new beginnings.

jumpstarts
for Life's
Challenges

Facing the Big Stuff and the
Little Stuff that
Feels Big

"Carry each other's burdens." —Galatians 6:2

Every day people die—sometimes unexpectedly and sometimes in the most tragic of circumstances. Every day people are diagnosed with debilitating, life-threatening illnesses. Every day people go hungry, while others are displaced from their homelands by war and natural disaster. Every day people lose their livelihoods. Every day people are betrayed, even used and abused, by people they should have been able to trust to love and care for them. Every day such happenings become forgotten headlines until somehow real faces get painted on the stick figures of statistics, until you or someone you know faces the big stuff head on.

What can you do to connect with someone you know who is facing the big stuff (or the little stuff that feels big) in life? What helps on the morning the diagnosis is cancer? How can you be there for someone who's lost their job or for a little person whose best friend died in a random shooting? Here are a few ideas for starters:

1. *Be alert.* It's not always easy for a person to tell you they are facing big challenges. It takes a great deal of courage to put some things into words. It may be too frightening to risk a hurtful response. Be on the lookout for signs of trouble—things like a sudden change in appetite, lack of interest in things that would normally have been interesting, isolation from family and friends, physical injury for which explanations are inadequate, lack of energy or other changes in a loved one that make you wonder if something might be very wrong. Even when someone shares their problem with you openly, know that you may be getting only the tip of the iceberg of distress that they are experiencing. Think also about the possibility of a problem behind the presenting problem. A child who has a stomachache before going to the babysitter's every day may not be a child who is ill. There may be problems at the day care or among the child's friends that need to be uncovered.

2. *Convey acceptance of the person.* Craig was a little boy who was marked by the troubled family from which he came. His teacher Betty was kind and accepting. Every day before her students arrived, she pictured the more difficult children from the class in her mind. She tried to visualize each child behaving in ways that would help them to be successful. Whenever Craig did something right, no matter how small or insignificant, she was quick to smile and offer kind words of affirmation. One day Craig left a carefully folded note on his teacher's desk. "Dear Teacher," it began. "Thank you for helping me when I got troubles. I got so much troubles."

Acceptance separates the person from their behavior which may be unacceptable. Acceptance says "I value you as a person, and I want to treat you with the dignity and respect with which every human being deserves to be treated." Acceptance is not incompatible with drawing the line on unacceptable behavior. Acceptance opens the way for the person experiencing the inappropriate behavior to see the other person who is behaving badly as a struggling human being in need of help. Acceptance opens the way for the person behaving in ways that are not acceptable to stop these behaviors and learn better ways of relating.

3. *Listen.* Good listeners are worth their weight in gold! They really want to understand what people are saying, so they give them their undivided attention and listen for both spoken and unspoken messages. They say things like, "That must have been so difficult for you." "You must have been very frightened." They know when a gentle touch would be appropriate and reassuring. Good listeners make it possible for people to explore and evaluate the alternatives open to them without telling them what to do.

Good listeners are comfortable with the full range of human emotion. When people are facing the big stuff, they may express any or all of the full range of feelings known to humankind. It can be hard to be on the other end of a full blast of the anger, resentment, frustration, hurt, disbelief, fear, overload, distress and more that may be expressed. Feelings are neither good nor bad. They just are. People dealing with serious difficulties need to know that it's okay to have feelings and that it's safe to share them with you if they would like. Feelings can be very scary when they have to be processed from within. Once they are out in the open, they can be considered more rationally and can lead to decisions more in keeping with personal values and the reality of the situation.

4. *Offer practical help.* When calamity strikes, the world suddenly feels turned upside down. Such disarray can be as difficult to deal with as the calamity itself. Faye's physician husband left her for a colleague at work. Until then, her days were filled with the children's activities, volunteer work and a whirlwind of the kinds of engagements a Mrs. Doctor would have. Now she awoke to juggle moving to a new location, looking for a job, fixing the toilet, finding a new pediatrician, arranging for child care and on and on. All the while, her personal world was in total disarray. There was the shock, the embarrassment, the devastation, the loneliness, the fear, the overload.

Faye tells of a Sunday morning when she thought she could not go one step further. Then the door bell rang. She opened the door, her three little girls peering around from behind her bathrobe. There was Annette standing on her porch. Dear Annette. Here she was again, not with packages of well-meaning advice, but with practical help! Cornflakes, some yummy looking cinnamon rolls, apple juice and milk spilled out of the top of her bag. Talking around Faye to the girls, Annette said, "So who'd like some breakfast? Come on, you three. We're going to my house. We're leaving your Mommy here to do whatever she wants for the day. We'll have you back home around 6:00 or whenever we've finished supper at the pizza place. What do you say we invite your Mommy along for that part?" Faye marks that day as the day life began again for her after the divorce.

5. *Help the family move from emergency mode to a sustainable routine.* When a family is facing the big stuff, everyone moves into emergency mode. There's usually a lot that needs doing, and the extra adrenaline flowing pumps up everyone's energy level to meet the demands. You can help by recognizing that no one can operate in emergency mode for long. Friends and family may be able to drop everything and help for awhile, but inevitably they become less available because they must return to their own responsibilities. Families in crisis sooner or later have to move into routines they can sustain over the long haul. You can help by expressing concern for family members who are pushing themselves too hard and by assisting the family in simplifying routines to a sustainable level until the crisis is past. You can organize the available support network of family and friends to spread the load over as many as possible. Be open and honest about how much you can do and about your limitations.

6. *Recognize when professional help is needed.* Friends and family are key to the support of people in trouble. But friends and family are best at being friends and family. They usually cannot help with the problems behind the problems. It is always appropriate to express concern for the physical and emotional well-being of someone. But when problems are serious, you can help best by connecting people with professionals with the expertise to really help them. You can identify the resources available in your community by calling the government agency responsible for various social services. A physician, a pastor, a teacher or a school counselor are also good places to begin to locate the different kinds of assistance that may be needed. It's not usually helpful to try to pressure someone into seeking professional help. One way to encourage them to do so is to refrain from playing the role of a professional yourself and to look for other appropriate ways to show you care.

7. Hang on to hope. When you're the one facing the big stuff, hope can be as elusive as a missing cat. But hope is the door to life beyond the crisis. Hope is born when friends and family believe in you and help you widen your focus to see the bigger picture. It feeds on hugs, mingled tears and acceptance just for who you are. For many, hope is rooted in faith in God who promises to work good even out of bad.

On Becoming
A Non-anxious
Presence

"Comfort one another." —*1 Thessalonians 4:18 (NKJV)*

As soon as Jay came through the front door, Debbie knew something was wrong. His face was tight and tired. His shoulders sagged as he let his bag drop to the floor and fingered silently through the mail on the table.

Jay didn't have days like this very often, but they happened. Of course Debbie wanted to know what was wrong, if there was anything she could do. But Jay had been able to tell her once before that he didn't need a barrage of questions from her in moments like these. It was good to know she was there and that she cared, but he just needed some space to sort things out. He would tell her about it when he was ready. Exercising deliberate restraint, Debbie touched his cheek as she passed by. "I'm glad you're home!" was all she said.

Counselors have long recognized that many of their clients come to them in need of someone who will listen and help them sort out what's going on in their lives. In addition to their expertise, counselors provide what's known in professional circles as "a non-anxious presence." A "non-anxious presence" is someone who is detached enough from the situation to not be experiencing anxiety at a personal level. Thus they are better able to help the persons more closely affected to understand what is causing the distress and to weigh the options open to them. Anyone who has experienced such a comforting human presence can appreciate its restorative effects.

When problems do not require the expertise of a professional, even a pet can be a wonderful non-anxious presence. Todd was a child with a lot of troubles. He didn't get along well with other children, and there were problems between his parents. Everyday he came home to an empty house until his parents returned from work—empty, that is, except for

Misty. Each afternoon when he came in from school, there was his little spaniel right at the door to greet him. She'd jump into his lap and lick his face with exuberant delight. When Todd was feeling low, angry at the world or whatever, he'd disappear with Misty for awhile and things seemed better somehow.

Pam's husband passed away after a long and painful illness. After a couple of months of visiting with her children, Pam decided it was time to brave life alone at home. Her health was good, and she liked her home. She had many friends in the small town where she lived and many meaningful activities to fill her days. But it was so quiet in the house. Nothing moved except Pam, and the loneliness from losing the love of her life nearly overwhelmed her. Pam's children felt her pain and asked her if she would like to have a dog. Pam had never been much of an animal person, but over time she relented.

When a small Yorkshire terrier named Pixie took up residence, however, loneliness gave way to mayhem! Pam described her feelings as akin to the emotions you'd experience the second after you had just dribbled peach juice down the front of your favorite blouse. If only you could turn back the clock just that one second! When a couple of months of diligent effort failed at taming this little bundle of energy, Pam in desperation offered her to a family with children. The parents, however, turned down her "gracious" offer. Pam did not know what to do. Her children suggested obedience school, and with patience and practice, Pixie slowly submitted to Pam's gentle control. Today the little Yorkie turned eight years old, and as you probably guessed, she and Pam are inseparable companions. They have their routines synchronized to perfection. No, Pixie's presence has not changed the reality that Pam misses her husband very much. But she is a boundless source of comfort and much joy.

Children have an incredible knack for comforting. One mother tells of her little Tina coming home late from school. "Where have you been, Tina?" her mom asked.

"Lisa dropped her best doll and it broke," explained Tina. "I stayed to help her."

"Oh, were you able to fix it? It was very kind of you to try."

"No Mom," Tina lamented. "I couldn't fix the doll. So I stayed to help her cry."

Pastor Dan was one of those persons people called about everything. He was just the one you wanted to talk to when you had a problem or something to share. Once he was visiting neighbors in the high rise apartment building next to his church. He knocked on the door of one resident, just to get acquainted. He met with a cold response, but was undaunted in his efforts to make a new friend. Upon finally gaining entrance, he found himself seated across from a very grumpy old lady who had nothing good to say about anyone, from the mayor to the maintenance man. Pastor Dan just listened as he always did, throwing in a few "Really!" and "Imagine that!" kind of comments along with lots of smiles. When the old woman's tirade slowed, Pastor Dan said he was delighted to have met her but he'd better be running along now. If it was okay with her, he'd be back later in the week with a loaf of his wife's fresh bread.

Pastor Dan would have thought little more about the episode had the woman's daughter not dropped by his office the following day. "Are you the pastor who visited my mother yesterday?" she inquired. Upon confirming that he was, the daughter introduced herself and promptly asked another question: "Whatever have you done to Mother?" Pastor Dan looked puzzled, so she continued. "My mother has been a totally different person since your visit!" the daughter went on incredulously. "She's actually been cheerful—not one of her usual qualities you might have guessed! And she says you're the best conversationalist in the whole wide world!"

There are times when we all need some comfort, when we need to be soothed. The *Chicken Soup for the Soul* book series has made it to the top of the bestseller list on this reality. The good news is that comforting can be a learned skill. What can the Misty's and the Pixie's and the Tina's and the Pastor Dan's teach us about being a great source of comfort, a soothing, non-anxious presence in the lives of those we love? In different cultures, people have their own ways of seeking and providing comfort. In one place it may be served up in a hot cup of herbal tea or a refreshing glass of cold water. In another, it may be expressed by bringing flowers or through music. But wherever you go, there are people who just seem to have a finely-tuned capacity for "being with" persons in need.

Some families have worked out their own means of comforting one another. In the Taylor family, they have a special comfort blanket. It all started when one of the kids was sick and refused to rest unless wrapped securely in this particular blanket. Along the way, the blanket has become a signal for the whole family. Whenever anyone feels sad or needs to be comforted, they go for the blanket. It sends the message, "Love me, reassure me, hug me, comfort me, be gentle with me because I'm hurting."

When Melissa senses her mom has had a difficult day, she makes gourmet hot chocolate for her in her prettiest teacup. Paula puts a note into her children's school bags when she knows they have a big exam coming up. Her notes let them know she has been listening to their hearts and that they are in her thoughts and prayers.

Richard and his wife longed to have a baby. For years they had hoped for a child, but Wendy did not become pregnant. Then, at last, they learned a baby was on the way. But their excitement was short-lived. By the end of one awful day when things began to go dreadfully wrong, Wendy had had a miscarriage. They had lost the baby they had so hoped for.

Richard was disappointed, but Wendy was so sad she didn't know what to do. Together they agreed that Wendy shouldn't cry alone. If she needed to cry, then Richard would be there. And if they couldn't manage the pain together, they would find a caring someone, perhaps with professional expertise, to help them process their tears. Years later, after they had three children, they realized how profoundly the miscarriage experience had affected them. They talked about how important it was to them that no one in the family be left to cry alone when they wished for someone to comfort them. Being together through their different sadnesses somehow brought them closer together as a family.

It's not always easy to live in this troubled world. But a touch of comfort can go a long way in soothing a hurting heart.

Anger:
Friend or Foe?

"Fathers, do not exasperate your children, instead, bring them up in the training and instruction of the Lord." —Ephesians 6:4

You've had a bad day, and you're exhausted. You worked as hard as you could at your job, but your boss still wanted more. The traffic on the way home was a nightmare, and you realize as you open the door that you forgot to stop for bread. You will have to go out again to the grocery store before you can pack school lunches for the following day. As you walk in, all four children are in a heap on the floor fighting over a tennis ball. One chair has been overturned, school books are scattered everywhere, and water is dripping off the edge of the end table where a cup has been knocked over. The emotional temperature in the room is high, very high! Many parents would start to yell at this point, or they would at least raise their voices—"just in order to be heard," right?

The kind of immediate response you will have to the above scenario will likely depend on your temperament and the way you have learned to manage your anger across your lifetime. Some might be able to size up the situation quickly and calmly. After determining that no one's life is in immediate danger, such parents are able to simply make their way through the mess to a quiet place where they can kick off their shoes and give themselves a few minutes to recover from a hard day. Even when they are upset, they seem able to remember that kids can usually work out their own problems among themselves.

Others types are more likely to jump right into the middle of the fray and put things right in their own way. They might physically disentangle the kids and send them off to the four corners of the house with a flurry of words. In the meantime, they'd noisily move about—setting the chair upright, mopping up the water, piling up the school books and venting their wrath on the offending tennis ball by throwing it forcefully into the trash. Though they know this is probably not the best moment for reasoning out a good solution or even for discipline, it's just too tempting to join the kids' battle and add more fuel to the emotional fire.

Still others might be more likely to punish with silence while going about the cleanup with an air of self-pity. Parents of this temperament might ignore the problem for the moment, but everyone in the family knows by experience that at some point they will pay for this fracas, big time! Unfortunately, the risk of damaging relationships runs just as high when anger is suppressed as it does when it is vented inappropriately.

So what do you do with all this emotionally charged energy? Will you use it to work for you or against you in your relationships? Can it really work for you? Someone has said that one of the primary distinguishing marks of a healthy family is the ability to handle anger in ways that promote growth and understanding in relationships. For many of us, this requires a whole new look at the emotion itself. Anger is an important part of the human emotional package. It is our anger energy that helps us protect ourselves when we are threatened. It is the part of us that responds with strong emotion when we see someone taking advantage or abusing another. It is anger energy that gives us the courage and strength to take action in their defense. Anger also provides an early warning signal that there are problems in a relationship that need to be addressed.

In order to make anger a friend in your family, one place to begin is to become more aware of the emotional temperature of your home atmosphere in general and each specific situation in particular. One father had the habit of throwing his hat in the kitchen door when he came home from work. If someone threw the hat back out the door, he knew there may be trouble brewing inside. If his hat was ignored or tossed back at him with a giggle, he knew he could enter with no worries. When a problem arises, first take a reading on the emotional temperatures of everyone involved, including yourself.

If you sense your own emotional temperature may negatively affect your behavior, you may wish to say something like, "We really need to talk about this. I'm sure we can find a way to work things out, but right now I'm afraid I might not be able to listen to you very well. I might say hurtful things. Can you give me some time to get my thoughts and feelings together while you do the same? Then we'll talk." It's always easier to move toward a good solution when everyone involved has had a chance to settle down. If your child needs calming, perhaps your spouse can soothe them. Remember that a few minutes can seem like an eternity to a child. Promise to talk soon, and make every effort to resolve the issue as quickly as you can do so responsibly.

To use up some of your excess emotional energy, it may help to sweep the floor, go for a walk around the block or kick leaves outside. These kinds of activities can help you gain control of your emotions so you can better address problems in ways that promote positive relationships. If such measures do not help, there is a good chance you may be experiencing more than the "garden variety" anger that all human beings know. Be good to yourself and your family. Seek the professional care of a trained counselor, pastor or physician before unresolved anger damages relationships further.

Helping children deal with their anger is very important. Small children can get very frustrated because they can't do everything they want to do. They don't always know how to ask for help either. It didn't take long for one mother to assess the situation when her son Jeffrey suddenly let out a shout and threw his shoe across the room. Jeff had been learning to tie his shoes and, for the most part, was experiencing success. But somehow this time he had gotten the lace into a tight knot which he could not undo despite his best efforts. Parents can help by anticipating children's needs and inabilities and trying to minimize their frustration without diminishing their self-respect and desire to "do it myself."

Somewhere between the canned soup aisle and the fresh vegetable displays, two-year-old Kelly went into an angry outburst. The market was busy, and her young mother was red with embarrassment. She had no idea what to do, but instinctively she picked up the screaming, kicking toddler and held her close. She just stood there in the aisle and enfolded Kelly in her arms, gently but firmly subduing her squirming. "It's all right, Kelly. Mommy's here," she whispered. Slowly the screams and resistance subsided. Kelly relaxed, and the angry outburst was over. Kelly learned that day that while Mommy would not allow the inappropriate behavior, she would be there to comfort her and keep her safe even when she felt out of control.

Terry came from a family where anger was often expressed in hurtful ways. Predictably, when he was angry he used the same destructive patterns that he had seen modeled at home. Sometimes he shouted, threw things, called the other children names, and even used bad language. None of these behaviors were winning him any friends on the playground. Terry's teacher Joyce saw his plight and wanted to help. Joyce knew that just telling Terry not to be angry would be futile. She decided on a step-by-step approach. She talked to Terry about the emotion of anger. She explained that it's a good emotion and helped him discover some of the good purposes it serves. She told him that there are helpful and hurtful ways to express anger. She helped him identify some of the hurtful ways he had been using.

Then she shared with him one idea for how he could improve his responses. Every time Terry got angry at school, Joyce affirmed him for something he had done better this time than the time before. Then she made one more suggestion for how he might improve the next time. Step-by-step Terry learned to express the feelings that led to his angry outbursts before they got out of control. He learned to use appropriate language and how to tell someone he was upset with them without attacking them. He learned that it is okay to feel angry, but that it is unacceptable to hurt people or destroy property. Terry is a fortunate child to have learned these important lessons early in life. Who in your family could benefit from Joyce's approach? Will you help?

The Art
of Forgiving

"Be kind and compassionate to one another, forgiving each other, just as in Christ God forgave you." —*Ephesians 4:32*

When Robert awoke, he could hardly move. He was buried in a shallow grave in the woods. His leg was badly cut and bleeding, and his head hurt terribly. He had no idea how long he'd been there or what had happened to him. With great effort, he crawled out of the ground in search of water. Fortunately, he was found by a passing hunter who helped him find his way to medical attention.

Robert was only thirteen when all this happened. After the attack he lived in fear. His face was badly scared. He was blind in one eye and could no longer run like other boys. No one ever knew who had attacked him or why. Time, however, eased the memories. In spite of his disabilities, he felt fortunate to have a good job and a loving family.

One day there came a knock at the door. A feeble old man in tattered clothes was standing on the doorstep when Robert answered. The stranger came immediately to the point. He had been the man who had attacked Robert years before after Robert's father refused to give him a job. All through the years, he had felt awful for hurting Robert and leaving him for dead. He had been so glad to learn that Robert survived.

Robert was shocked. He'd never seen this man before. Many times when he was young he had thought about what he wished he could do to pay him back for the life-changing injuries. But now, as he stood there before him, all Robert could see was a miserable, tormented old man who had been plagued for years with guilt for his crime. As Robert lifted his eyes to meet those of his attacker, he came to the realization that the old man had suffered consequences far greater than his own. He had no family, no rewarding career. He had come to ask for nothing. He only wanted to say he was sorry, hoping he could put an end to the misery with which he had lived every minute since that fateful day. He wanted to die in peace.

Robert found himself welcoming the old man into his home, feeding him, giving him some of his own clothes and assuring him that although the attack had had its lasting effects on his life, he had forgiven his attacker long years before. Robert and his family continued to befriend the old man, visiting him often. When he finally died, it was Robert who was by his side.

It's not easy to say you're sorry when you have hurt someone, and it's not easy to let go of the hurt when someone has caused you pain. Certainly Robert's story is extraordinary. Is forgiveness for regular people who want to forgive, but for whom the release from pain and hatred seems elusive? The answer is yes. Understanding more about forgiveness can help. Here are a few things to think about when you're trying to be a forgiver:

❧ Think about the times when you've done something hurtful and been forgiven by another person. How did that feel? If others have been big enough and kind enough to forgive you, ask yourself whether you can pass the gift on in an act of forgiveness. The more we sense how much we have been forgiven, the more we see our responsibility to forgive others. Be willing to make the first move. Knowing that you have forgiven already is a powerful invitation to the wrongdoer to acknowledge their wrongdoing and come to you in repentance.

❧ Don't take responsibility for things that weren't your fault. Forgiveness is not about making excuses for another's wrong or blaming yourself for another person's decision to behave in hurtful ways. While it is good to be willing to take responsibility for your part in the breakdown of a relationship, there are times when the problem belongs to the other person and you may not have responsibility to bear. Talking with a pastor or counselor can help you sort this out. Particularly when abuse and violence are present in a relationship, experts are clear in their understanding that nothing victims say or do "causes" an abuser to abuse them. Abuse is a deliberate choice on the part of one person to control another person. Until an abuser can be helped to take full responsibility for their actions and stop the abusive behavior, the safety of all concerned must be the first priority. Of course victims are not perfect, but relationship issues cannot be dealt with until the abuse has stopped.

❧ Remember, forgiveness is a process, not the act of a moment. It begins with the acknowledgement of deep hurt. It moves the wounded one through feelings of anger and hatred and eventually leads them to release the wrongdoer from their resentment and punishment. As we are more and more able to see the wrongdoer as a broken person in need of grace, we forgive as we choose again and again to respond graciously.

◢ Know that feelings of having forgiven often take a long time to come. Louis Smedes, Christian author of *The Art of Forgiving*,[1] offers this encouragement: None of us is an expert at forgiving. No matter how old we are, because we are human, we are all beginners. Most of us go through the forgiveness cycle (forgiving today—hating again tomorrow—and forgiving again the next day) many times before the forgiveness process is finally complete. But all along the way, we are forgivers if we choose to seek the path of forgiveness rather than the path of retribution.

◢ Recognize that though forgiveness is a healing balm that can ease the pain of hurtful wrongdoing, all of the consequences cannot necessarily be removed. Human beings don't forgive and forget. As Smedes reminds us, only the senile forget. Scars often remain, though they no longer give rise to the terrible pain that they once did. Relationships may or may not be able to be restored. But forgiveness can make it possible for us to grow from the experience and to move on to new beginnings, free from the destructive forces of hatred and retaliation.

◢ Learn to distinguish between the act of forgiveness and reconciliation. It's important to remember that though they are often spoken of in the same breath, they are not synonymous. Forgiveness has two phases. In the first phase, forgiveness is a choice on the part of the person who has been wronged to release the wrongdoer from their revenge, retaliation, resentment and other forms of punishment. This first phase of forgiveness can eventually draw the sting from the wounded place. It opens the way for the inner healing of the person who has been wronged, irregardless of the response of the wrongdoer. This phase of forgiveness also provides a powerful call to repentance for the person who has wronged another. It conveys the good news that the fountain of forgiveness is already flowing in their direction from the heart of the person they have hurt so deeply.

Forgiveness can only come full circle when there is sincere repentance on the part of the wrongdoer. Know the earmarks of true repentance. Wrongdoers who are truly repentant take full responsibility for the wrong they have committed. They do not minimize the pain they have caused, and they do not offer excuses. In every way possible, they make restitution for lost or damaged property. Another hallmark of true repentance is a willingness to pay for any treatment necessary to help the hurting one heal from the painful experience. Genuine repentance also leads the wrongdoer to cooperate fully with available treatment, to stop the hurtful behavior and to make deliberate changes in the way they relate to others so as to avoid causing further pain in the future.

Only when there is evidence of true repentance is it safe for reconciliation to be considered. Sometimes there has been so much damage to the relationship that reconciliation simply is not possible. In such cases, individuals and families may need help to grieve the loss of a significant relationship for which they had great hopes, only to be devastatingly disappointed.

A wise man once said that a person who can't forgive another's wrong, wrongs himself twice. It's true that hatred and resentment often hurt us more, in the end, than the original event. Ill will in our hearts can destroy our own happiness and peace of mind, while it will likely have little effect on the person who has wronged us. Forgiveness is always a miracle of grace. It requires the very best inside each human being to offer such a gift. Can you offer this incredible gift to someone you know today?

ENDNOTE

1 Lewis B. Smedes, *The Art of Forgiving* (Nashville, Tenn.: Moorings, 1996).

Winning Big

"Each of you should look not only to your own interests, but also to the interests of others." —*Philippians 2:4*

Shirley hung up the phone in disbelief. Dale had known for weeks that tonight was the final dress rehearsal for the community Christmas choir performance. He had promised to watch the kids and agreed that the family van would be available so she could give several of her friends a ride. What made him think now that he could just call at the last minute and announce that he would be working late and couldn't take care of the kids? And, of course, the van wouldn't be available either. Why did she always have to take up the slack when his boss loaded on the work? If Dale really cared about her, he'd just stand up to the boss and tell him he already had plans for tonight!

Dale sat at his desk, still smarting from Shirley's tirade. He couldn't see why a dress rehearsal was necessary anyway. Shirley could sing the music in her sleep. How hard could it be to stand in her place on the stage? Why should her choir practice take priority over his work? After all, it was *their* livelihood! And besides, she could get a sitter, and someone else could surely drive.

Conflict is inevitable in close relationships. It was a wise observer of human behavior who quipped, "If they say there is no conflict in their marriage, either they're lying or one of them is dead!" The good news is that there's nothing inherently bad about conflict. The way conflict is handled, however, will largely determine the quality of any relationship.

People take many stances toward conflict. Some want to *avoid* it at all costs. Couples are often in this mode early in their marriage. They dream of a perfect relationship, and conflict threatens that dream. The safest path seems to be denial and avoidance. She wants to go shopping again tonight; he hates shopping. But what can he do but go shopping and pretend to like it, because going shopping, it seems, will keep the dream alive.

Others acknowledge that conflict exists, but they *withdraw* from it, refusing to talk about the issue and hoping it will go away. Resentments build because there is no apparent path to a satisfactory resolution. Ross was a physician who was used to giving orders and having many people at his beck and call. At home, his wife Ginger was not willing to operate in this mode. Ross barked out his orders, but his wife's response was always the same. "As you wish dear." As nice as the response looks in print, however, insincerity dripped from her lips. It was clear from her tone that she had no intention of acting on his wishes. But the problem itself was never discussed, and the marriage disintegrated.

Still others *yield* every time conflict arises. Yielding, as a primary conflict resolution style, may initially reflect a genuine concern for others and desire to cooperate. It may also, however, signal a fear of confrontation and lack of appropriate assertiveness skills. Yielding may appear to work for awhile, but usually the person whose needs and desires are continually being sacrificed grows disenchanted and begins to feel used by the other person. Eventually, yielding leads to disillusionment and the breakdown of the relationship.

Some people's conflict resolution style grows out of their belief that no one is going to look out for them, so they have to look out for themselves. They feel they need to *win* at all costs. In reality, when a person forces their way at the expense of the needs and desires of others, no one really wins, and the relationship is often a casualty.

Some try to meet others halfway. This *compromise* approach appears on the surface to have merit. He gives a little, she gives a little—sounds pretty good. Too often, however, it leads to keeping score in a relationship. In this style, people often maintain memory banks as big as an elephant's. More often than not, each has the sense that things are never quite even up.

Certainly there are situations in which any of the above styles might be workable, at least for the short term. In a crisis, there may not be time or energy for anything more than avoidance or withdrawal. There are many times when one is genuinely able to yield to the desires of another, to give their wishes to them as a gift of love. Compromise is at least an attempt to be fair and to consider the desires of others. But all of these approaches come with serious limitations that can negatively impact relationships.

Dr. David Mace and his wife Vera, co-founders of the Association of Couples for Marriage Enrichment, have worked with thousands of couples in counseling and marriage strengthening programs over several decades. They were keenly interested in discovering the factors that separate couples whose relationships grow and deepen over time from couples whose relationships stagnate and break down. One of the key factors that characterized good marriages was the couple's ability to use conflict positively in their relationship. In such marriages, the Mace's observed a commitment to a *collaborative* approach to conflict resolution. This approach seeks solutions that are satisfactory to all concerned and have the best potential for working long term.

Think about the mode in which you usually operate in your family. You may already be a collaborative problem solver. Then again, maybe there are some fresh ideas here for you. Try this step-by-step guide to a collaborative process that has helped many couples to find winning solutions for all concerned:

Step 1: Seek to resolve concerns, grievances and potential conflict situations as they occur. One good business woman thinks of it as "keeping short accounts." If circumstances prevent you from working to resolve the problem immediately, then agree upon a time in the near future when you will.

Step 2: Use your best communication skills to listen and share. Attack the problem, not your partner. Think of yourselves as working together for the good of your relationship, rather than fighting against each other.

Step 3: Identify the needs of each person involved in the conflict. A "need" is a compelling emotional or psychological concern that underlies the immediate conflict. David Augsburger, in his book *Caring Enough to Confront*, explains this stage: "Try on your brother's skin. Listen until you hear his point of view. Then get inside it. See how it fits for size. See how it feels to be there where he or she is. See what love is asking you to do."[1]

Remember Shirley and Dale's conflict over the use of the van? For Shirley, identifying needs will mean recognizing that Dale feels responsible to hold a job in order to provide income for the family. He wants to maintain his relationship with his boss. He may also feel awkward about asking a co-worker to drive far out of his way to give him a ride home.

For Dale, identifying Shirley's needs will mean understanding that she is at home with children most of the time and really looks forward to being with other adults. It will mean feeling Shirley's embarrassment at the prospect of missing this important choir practice and going back on her commitment to provide the transportation she promised her friends.

Step 4: Ask yourself if this is a situation in which you can give the other person what they want without jeopardizing significant needs of your own. Often the exercise of getting in touch with one another's deeper needs will lead to a desire to accommodate the other out of love. Many conflicts can be resolved at this step, but it may be necessary to revisit the solution if the partner doing the accommodating begins to feel unhappy about having done so.

Step 5: Generate all the alternative possibilities you can think of which might lead to a solution that both can accept. Try for at least 20. Write them down. Be creative. Don't rule out even the ones that appear at first to be unworkable. They may eventually become a part of your best idea. Draw everyone involved into this brainstorming phase. Sometimes it can be helpful to think of "improving" the situation rather than "solving" it.

Step 6: Evaluate the alternative solutions. Discard any that are unacceptable to either of you, and pick one or combine several to provide a solution that everyone can agree on and that meets the needs of everyone concerned.

Step 7: Plan a time for reviewing your solution. Many times what looks like a good solution in the beginning will turn out to have some hitches. Make time to talk about how your solution is working and make the necessary adjustments so everyone continues to feel good about the course you have taken.

Couples whose relationships are flourishing around the globe confirm that this really does work. It's worth the time and energy to go through the steps if you want to "win big" in your relationship.

ENDNOTES

1 David W. Augsburger, *Caring Enough to Confront* (Ventura, Calif.: Regal Books, 1980), 119-120.

jumpstarts
for Parenting

Parenting
for Life

"My son, pay attention to what I say; listen closely to my words
. . . for they are life to those who find them." —*Proverbs 4:20, 22*

Little Philip pulled himself up to a full stand, hanging tightly onto his mom's knees. He paused a moment, wobbled a little, then put out his left foot. Gathering courage and concentrating hard, he finally let go and took his first step! It was only a short step before he was on his bottom again, but it was definitely a step in the right direction. Rose picked her little boy up and hugged him. Then she stood him on his feet again and encouraged him to take the few steps into his daddy's arms.

Like most parents, after the initial excitement of those first steps wears off, Rose and Alan wondered why they'd ever encouraged Philip to walk in the first place. Life was so much easier when he stayed put! Now nothing was safe. Philip was into everything the minute they turned their backs. No more leaving him for a minute to fetch something from another room. By the time they were back, he'd have found a book to chew, pulled a vase off a shelf or wandered too close to the stairway for comfort.

It seems that almost as soon as our children are born, we have to start letting them go. At first it's only into another's arms for a quick hug or to leave them with a friend when we want to go out. When they're small, we make all the choices about where they'll go. But as soon as they can move about on their own, they begin to lead their own lives.

One thing that wise parents keep in mind is that children are not for satisfying their own needs and desires. Rather, the goal is to bring up children who will one day be able to manage their own lives without adults there to coach them all the time. To realize this goal, children will need to learn to make good choices. They'll need age-appropriate freedom to make decisions and to learn from the consequences. Preparing them for such big responsibility is what parenthood is all about. It begins the day they are born.

Corrie was just three when a neighbor observed this brilliant scenario. Her mother Lani was thinking long range as she carefully taught her, even at this tender age, how to make a good choice. It was time for Corrie to get dressed for the day. Her mother told her she could choose what she would like to wear, but helped her think about what she would need to remember to make a good choice. What kind of a day was it? A warm day. What would they be doing today? They would be going to the park. With that in mind, Corrie ran off to choose her outfit.

A few minutes later she was back, ready for Mommy to button up the new dress her grandma had just sent her for church. "You really like your new church dress, don't you," Lani smiled. "But let's think if it's a good dress for today. "What kind of a day is it outside?" Mother asked.

"A warm day," Corrie confirmed.

"Your new dress is for a warm day; you are right about that. But what will you be doing today, Corrie?"

"Going to the park."

"Is this a good dress for playing on the swings and in the sandbox at the park? What if you get mud on it or tear it on the seesaw?" Corrie agreed it wasn't a good dress for going to the park. Mother helped her take it off and sent her back to her room to try again. After a couple of tries, she emerged with a pair of jeans and a tee shirt. Lani affirmed that the outfit was perfect for a warm day and for going to the park. Already Corrie was learning to make good decisions.

While in one sense you can't begin too soon to develop these important life skills, children mature on different schedules and do best when allowed to grow at their own pace. If given too much responsibility too early, children can get hurt or become unnecessarily anxious and fearful. On the other hand, parents may need to protect children who want to rush into independence too soon, before they're able to handle the situation safely. Over-eager children may need some gentle restraint, while the cautious bystanders may need some gentle encouragement to get involved and try new things.

The Baker's had three children. The oldest and youngest were reasonably adventurous, but Kimber, their middle child, was always quite cautious. His parents felt concerned for him because he seemed always to be sitting on the sidelines rather than engaging in the fun. One day the family went out in a long flat boat called a punt that's pushed along using a pole. Everyone wanted to have a go except Kimber. Mom and Dad had a hunch he'd probably enjoy the experience, so they put up some encouragement. Dad promised a special treat for everyone who tried punting the boat. Even

Mom had a go, and soon Kimber took his turn. He did like it and was quite good at it too. That day, Kimber put one more experience into his memory bank to confirm that it's worth trying new things because sometimes it can be good fun.

Teaching children to take responsibility for their own actions is very important. Children need to learn that freedom comes with accountability, choices with consequences. One family has what it calls their "leave no footprints rule." It comes from the North American Indian commitment to preserving the earth. Early inhabitants prided themselves in moving through the forest and countryside without disturbing nature or leaving any trace behind to mar the landscape. This family has adapted this rule to preserve relationships. It gives each member responsibility for cleaning up their own "messes," whether it's telling your brother you're sorry for being cross or cleaning up the kitchen after you make a sandwich. The idea is to leave no family business unfinished.

It's important to teach our children the life skills they will need for independent living—things like how to manage money, cook, do laundry and shop for clothing. It's just as important to teach the life skills for interdependence. Interdependence is about knowing how to live with others in ways that encourage and strengthen the family and community. These life skills include things like knowing how to work well with others; learning to be trustworthy, honest and loyal and how to recognize these qualities in others; and developing the capacity for commitment and intimacy. The best way to pass on to children the life skills they will need is to live them out in our own lives and to make them as attractive as possible to our children. It helps to keep a clear vision in mind of the kind of adult you want your child to be. That picture will be your guide as you gently bring your child back to the road that leads to the good life whenever they stray to one side or the other.

A parent once wrote this letter to his child:

"My dear child,

"I haven't been able to give you much in the way of material things, but there are some special gifts I want you to have that are worth more than money. I determined from the moment you were born to give you these precious gifts long before you were old enough to know their value.

"The first gift is love. I have always loved you with all of my heart. I believe the most important thing you can give any other human being is your love. I want you to know you will always be loved, no matter what.

"The second gift I want for you is wisdom. Wisdom is more precious than many riches. It will help you look after all the other gifts.

"The third is peace of mind. I want you to know the joy of being content with what you have and living by values that lead to the good life for yourself and for others.

"The fourth gift is happiness. Happiness can be found, but contrary to what you might think, it is found in making others happy rather than seeking happiness for yourself.

"The fifth is intimacy. I want you to know the joys of close relationships and how to touch the lives of others deeply and be touched in return. I want you to know the security and safety of commitment to family that has made my life complete.

"I hope you will treasure these gifts. They are the best that I can give.

"With all my love, Dad."

Filling
Love Cups

"Love is as strong as death. . . . It burns like blazing fire, like a mighty flame. Many waters cannot quench love; rivers cannot wash it away." —Song of Songs 8:6, 7

Mrs. Carson was a single parent. She had to work three jobs to support her family, but she had plenty of love—and love for her was an action verb! Even though she couldn't choose the best of neighborhoods to raise her family, Mrs. Carson wisely made her boys an offer they couldn't turn down. For every book they read and wrote a reading report, she would give them a sum of money. It would keep her boys safely occupied and learning at the same time, she reasoned. When she received their reports, she paid them the promised money with a smile and a pat on the back for good measure. It wasn't until years later that they realized she had never been able to read a word they'd written. Today one of her sons is Dr. Benjamin Carson, an internationally renowned brain surgeon. It would have been so easy for young Ben to have gone the way of many neighborhood youth. But his mother's love was a powerful force in his life, and it was love with a purpose for his good.

Marta loved her children too, but she didn't know much about showing love. She'd been brought up in a troubled family where "I love you" just wasn't something people said. The only time she could remember being touched by her dad was when he punished her for doing something he didn't like. Now that she was older, Marta wanted to believe that deep down her parents loved her. They had worked hard to provide food and clothing and to send her to school. But Marta knew she wanted more for her children. She wanted them to grow up knowing for sure that they were loved. She just didn't know where to start. The words "I love you" sounded so strange when she said them. When she tried to give one of the kids a hug, her body felt stiff and clumsy, and her arms never seemed to be in the right place.

Perhaps you find it hard to say "I love you." Practice whispering it quietly to yourself until it comes off your tongue easier. You may decide to write a personal letter to each of your children, perhaps on their birthday, telling them how glad you've always been that they are your child, or what a special day it was the day they were born, or what makes them more precious to you than all the money in the world.

It can be a harsh world out there. You only have to be too little, too big, too clever, or to have ears that stick out to become a target for teasing. Even if you quite fit into the crowd by appearance, only one child wins the race, only one or two make the top grade. Children need a family where they can feel free to be themselves, without the pressures of school, friends and society. They need a place that's safe from being teased and hurt, and where they know they are loved, no matter how they look or perform. That's real love, strong love. A love that watches for signs that someone's "love cup" might be running a little low and tops it up with a word of affirmation or a squeeze about the shoulders. A love that fortifies children for a world where criticism and rejection abound. A love that's always there and can be depended on for comfort, support, safety and encouragement when everything else has gone wrong.

Kim was born with a disability. Her feet and hands were misshapen. She found it hard to walk and do the simplest things. She had countless operations, and still she couldn't see how she would ever live independently. She had missed years of schooling, but she had one thing no one could ever take away from her. She knew her parents loved her and would be there for her no matter what the circumstances. With their help and support, she persisted through difficult physical therapy treatment. Progress was slow, but with determination and parents who believed in her, she managed to overcome her disabilities. She learned to walk. She learned to use her hands to take care of herself. Her dad was so proud of her that he fixed up a used car for her to drive as a surprise for her eighteenth birthday. "A person who's going to live on her own has to have a way to get around!" he said proudly.

Empowering love sends the message to your children that you will always love them. Nothing they can ever do will cause you to stop loving them. Such love offers the confidence they need to try new things. It is also there to help them pick up the pieces of failure and meld them into a learning experience. Many families offer only an "I-will-love-you-if love." This kind of love sends the message that love comes only in exchange for doing what their parents want them to do, behaving perfectly or getting top scores. In reality, this kind of "love" shouldn't be called love at all. It leaves children struggling to please but feeling—often for a life time—that they are never good enough.

Jon was the youngest of six children. It seemed his special talent was for finding new ways to get into trouble. He would tease the dog until it barked like crazy. He'd practice his juggling with eggs from the henhouse. He persisted in climbing trees in his good school pants and floated his shoes down the river. His father Adam was always having to look for him and send him back to his chores. No discipline his parents tried seemed to work.

One day his father Adam tried to put himself in Jon's shoes. Jon was the youngest child in a busy household. As Adam thought about it, he suddenly came to the realization that the only time Jon ever got any attention was when he was being bad. The only time father and son spent alone together was when Adam was disciplining his son. No wonder Jon was always in trouble. The two parents decided this called for a complete shift in tactics. Adam and his wife began to look out for the times when their son did something right. At first, they could only find a few things, but they affirmed him no matter how small the effort or sign of improvement.

Adam began to look for opportunities to spend time one-on-one with the boy. He took him with him into town when he went to get the truck fixed. He let him hang around his workbench while he fixed his lawnmower. He even found time for an hour or two of football on the weekend. Slowly, imperceptibly, Jon was being transformed into a different boy. The life-changing power of love was doing its work.

Clyde recalls even in old age how eagerly he waited for his mother to come home from work. All he wanted was to hold her hand as she walked up to the house. Children blossom when they feel that, even for a few minutes or better yet an hour or so a day, they are your highest priority. They need to know that their needs and wishes are the most important things in the world to you right then. Even if you can only spend small amounts of time with each of them, guard that time as if it were your most precious possession.

Kelly was teaching her friend Nelma to knit. One afternoon as they were knitting together, she noticed that her friend had made a mistake. Thinking Nelma would be discouraged when she discovered her mistake, Kelly waited until her friend was asleep to take out the rows back to the mistake and to knit them again, mistake corrected. In the morning Nelma picked up her knitting, looked puzzled for a minute, then laughed. "You fixed my mistake, didn't you Kelly." Kelly confessed, mumbling that she didn't think Nelma even knew it was there. "Oh, I knew it was there, all right" Nelma smiled. "I just told myself what my dad always told me. 'It will never be seen from a galloping horse!' I guess he freed me up to make a mistake or two along the way. That may be the most important lesson he ever taught me. Thanks though. You're sweet!"

Plan a time in the next week to spend at least a few moments with each of your children. Affirm them for the things you appreciate about them and all the ways they contribute to the family circle. Let them know you notice their efforts in areas where they are struggling to grow. This is love. Remember, love is the most fundamental need of the human heart. It's a gift you can afford to give!

Receiving Worn
Silver and Gold
Jewelry

"He who answers before listening, that is his folly and his shame." —*Proverbs 18:13*

Maria was making dinner when Antonia arrived home from school. Her daughter came in the door chattering about her day, her friends, what they did on the way home, her spelling test and on and on. All the while, Maria was busy cooking beans and chopping vegetables, trying to get the meal ready. Her mind was divided between her daughter, the kitchen and the market where she still needed to pick up a few things before she could finish her preparations. She threw in a few "Mmmm's" and "Really's" and a well-placed "That's nice." She was feeling quite good about the way her daughter talked to her about everything. Then Antonia finished off with, "So what do you think, Mommy?"

Maria stopped chopping and looked up sheepishly. "Mmmm. You got me! Perhaps I'd have some good ideas if you told me that story all over again." Oops! Maria hadn't really been listening. Is there a parent alive who hasn't been caught in such a circumstance? Who hasn't been tempted to try to do at least two things at once? Certainly any parent worth her salt can handle a child's prattle and something else important at the same time! So how well have you been listening to your children recently? Try this simple test.

How many of these questions can you answer?

- 🌿 Can you name your child's best friends?
- 🌿 What is your child's favorite subject at school?
- 🌿 What is his least favorite subject?
- 🌿 What would your child most like to do with you if you had a free day together?
- 🌿 What challenges is your child facing at the moment?

- What are your child's favorite foods?
- What does your child want to do when he or she leaves school?
- What do you do that annoys your child the most?

Listening and keeping your child talking to you go hand in hand. If your teenager suspects you aren't interested or willing to give them your undivided attention, the chances are they won't bother to talk to you. They'll just be off to find a friend who's more interested. An anonymous poet put it this way:

I will present you
parts of myself.
Slowly,
if you are patient and tender,
I will open drawers
that mostly stay closed,
and bring out places and people and things,
sounds and smells,
loves and frustrations,
hopes and sadness
that have been grabbed off
in chunks
and found lying in my hands.
They have eaten their way into my memory,
carved their way into my heart.
Altogether—you or I will never see them.
They are me.
If you regard them lightly,
deny that they are important,
or worse, judge them,
I will quietly, slowly
begin to wrap them up
in small pieces of velvet,
like worn silver and gold jewelry,
tuck them away
in a small wooden chest of drawers,
and close.

Why is listening so important? Paul Tillich offered this answer: "The first duty of love is to listen." Listening says "You are important to me, and

I care about you. I value you, therefore the things you want to share with me are important, too."

Listening is also one of the best ways to discover a child's needs. Maybe they're afraid of a bully at school or having difficulty learning their multiplication tables. Perhaps there is a lot of pressure on them to do something they don't want to do, like smoking or doing drugs. Maybe your child is looking for an opportunity to tell you they need to use you as an excuse for why they can't go to a party where they know there won't be any adults present.

Listening also helps parents understand how their children are thinking about current issues, what interests them and the beliefs they hold that are important to them. Wise parents listen first and listen well. As the ancient wise man said, it is folly to speak without hearing the whole story first.

Lennie had a hard time following his young son's monologues about school. Sammy skipped from one tale to another so fast, and there were so many names. Lennie was always struggling to piece together who was who, and who did what, where and when. One day they had an idea. They got a large piece of paper and together Lennie and Sammy drew a picture of Sammy's classroom. Then they drew in the desks and put each child's name in their place. Next to their names they wrote other things Sammy knew about them—like where they lived, what they were good at, and what they looked like—to help Lennie get better acquainted with his son's friends. After that, whenever Sammy wanted to talk to his dad about school, they got out the big piece of paper. With it in front of them, the stories made ever so much more sense to Dad. After awhile, Lennie was able to connect names with faces when Sammy's friends came over to play or when he met them at church and school functions. Meanwhile, Sammy gave Lennie much higher marks for listening!

A current national study in the United States marks "connectedness" as the single most important factor in lowering the incidence of adolescent involvement in behaviors that put their health and well-being at risk. Kids feel connected when significant adults in their lives know the issues they consider important right now. Connectedness means knowing their friends and something important about each one of them. It means remembering your child has a big spelling test. It means being available in case they want your help to review or just to keep them in your thoughts and prayers as they take the test. Connectedness also means assurance that you will be around afterward either to celebrate or to comfort depending on the results.

Connectedness means becoming adept at listening between the lines, listening for significant patterns in the stories they tell that may indicate a concern. For example, are your child's stories from school always about being alone? Are they having problems with a particular teacher or feeling afraid about something? If so, you may need to explore what might be going on with professionals and others who can help—like your child's pediatrician, the school counselor, the teachers involved, other parents—all in the interest of a better understanding of your child's world.

George's dad thought that children were to be seen and not heard. Consequently, George grew up believing that his opinions and ideas weren't worth discussing, that nobody would ever be interested in what he had to say. George was hurt deeply by his father's attitude. He would hardly ever speak, and when he did, he could barely get the words out of his mouth. Fortunately, George met Hilary. She loved George's quiet ways and was patient enough with his stammering to discover how bright and interesting he really was. In her love, his confidence grew. Eventually George became a teacher. He had learned by experience that all children need adults who are interested enough to encourage them to share their ideas. As he listened to his students, he was never disappointed by their fresh insights and stories. Fortunate is the adult whose attention unlocks their imaginations.

Robert discovered that his children always wanted to talk at bedtime. At first he felt annoyed. Loose tongues seemed a good ploy to stay up beyond bedtime. But Robert learned to treasure these bedside chats as some of the best moments he shared with his children. In those few minutes each night they would talk of things they seldom spoke about at other times. As he would rub their backs or their legs sore from running, out would flow a steady stream of worries, joys and dreams. These night-time rituals became precious opportunities to bond with each of his children that Robert wouldn't exchange for anything.

Here's one parent's recipe for good listening:

Take one chair, sit down and look comfortable.

Take one mind and empty it of all your own worries and thoughts. (You can always have them back later if you still want them.)

Use two ears and one mouth, only in these proportions!

Take one child with something to say, and concentrate completely on them.

Add plenty of eye contact, a few hugs and a backrub to taste.

Flavor with pure extract of "Mmmm" and "Really."

Test every few minutes, checking that you've got the right message and helping your child find ways to communicate everything they want to say.

Watch for body language, and listen for important repeated messages and patterns.

Garnish with smiles.

Note: This dish needs to be freshly prepared just before dining. It cannot be dried, pickled or served up as leftovers.

If you are looking for entree into your child's inner world, learning to receive "worn silver and gold jewelry" is an important key. Help them not to "tuck them away . . . and close." If you listen when they're seven, they might still be talking and listening to you when they're seventeen!

Talking So
Kids Will Listen

"Pleasant words are a honeycomb, sweet to the soul and healing to the bones."—Proverbs 16:24

Who of us doesn't understand the urgency in the voice of the ancient wise man as he exhorts his sons to listen to him! "Listen my sons, to a father's instruction; pay attention and gain understanding. I give you sound learning, so do not forsake my teaching. When I was a boy . . ." (Proverbs 4:1-3). The weight of the consequences associated with the important life decisions confronting their children often looms large before parents. Parents long to spare them the painful lessons of the school of hard life experience. Over and over the wise man repeats himself, punctuating his exhortations with obvious concern: "Pay attention!" "Listen well!" "Do not forsake your mother's teaching!" "Keep my commands in your heart, for they will prolong your life many years!" If the truth is known, we parents have probably repeated ourselves too, and with the same sense of urgency. The question is, are our children listening? Is there a way to talk that will increase the likelihood we will be heard?

Sid was a shouter. He would stand in the middle of the floor and holler for his children to come this minute and do this or that. Mostly they just ignored him, at least until he was on his third or fourth yell. His wife Shirley was by nature a very calm and quiet person. Yelling was not her style. Rather, she preferred to walk over to where a child was and quietly make her request. It was like her to politely ask for a few minutes of someone's time to convey any concerns that she had or to work out the responsibilities for this week's chores. Sid could never understand why the children obeyed Shirley much more quickly than they did him. It was hard for him to imagine how her soft voice commanded more attention that his loud booming.

Whenever Ted's children approached him with a request, his first reaction was always to say "no." He would issue a very definite "no," but without any explanation. When you think about it, "no" is not a very helpful thing to say all by itself. What does "no" mean? Does it mean "not now," or "never"? Are the parents saying "no" because the request is totally unacceptable, because it's inconvenient, because Dad's too busy to consider an answer just now, or because Mom really doesn't care about her daughter's happiness?

Fred had a different approach. He tried never to say "no." He might say "Not right now, but we could do that tomorrow evening. Will that work?" Or, "It may not be such a good idea to climb that tree because I know there's a wasp's nest half way up, right where you'd need to grab hold of the branch." Or, "I'll need some time to think about that one." If parents have to say "no," they really need to explain why if at all possible. Without an explanation, a flat "no" can sound unreasonable to a child and can lead to a great deal of frustration and resentment.

Dave was very proud of his yard. His grass was always trimmed to perfection. Around the entire perimeter he nurtured a perennial garden that was the talk of the town. The tall stalks of larkspur were beautifully accented by the contrasting reds of the poppies and bright clumps of daisies and lavender. Prolific pinks provided the groundcover at the grass's edge. There was never a weed in sight.

One day Dave bought a new tool for edging the grass. Son Martin watched his dad for awhile and then asked if he could give the new tool a go. Dad showed him just how to do it, but warned as he passed it over, "Now Son, just be sure you don't damage any of my flowers!" Martin really enjoyed yard work. It was a change of pace from his studying, and as he stood back to survey his work, he thought he had done a pretty good job for a first time use of a new tool. He hoped his dad would be pleased.

Just then Dave came back around the corner and noticed immediately that Martin had chopped into a couple of bedding plants at the grass's edge, snipping off a handful of blossoms that now lay scattered on the grass. Straight away he started in on Martin. "Look what you've done! Didn't I tell you to be careful not to cut into my flowers. Well, my garden's ruined, and just in time for the garden tour next week. I should have known better than to let you anywhere near my flowers. You are such a disaster when it comes to yard work. Get along inside. I'll have to see what I can do to fix this mess. It will be a cold day at the Equator before I let you near my garden again!"

Mom heard Dad shouting and came to see what was happening. She hardly noticed the damaged flowers amongst the many lovely blossoms.

She smiled at Martin and thanked him for his work. Then she quietly knelt beside her husband and began to trim up the injured plants, tucking in the rough edges and smoothing away the evidence of damage. When Dave had had awhile to simmer down, he looked at his wife with deep sadness in his eyes. He knew he had done much more damage by his response than Martin had ever done. And damage to relationships takes much longer to heal than gardens. Mom knew what he was thinking and patted him on the shoulder. "I know how much pride you take in your garden, Dave. It's hard sometimes to remember we're raising both children and flowers. I'm sure Martin will be open to your apology. He loves you very much and really wants to please you."

When you're upset and angry at your children, the natural human response is to point the finger of blame or to lash out in a tirade of harsh words. Janie had reached the end of her rope. "Do you always have to have a drink while you run my computer? Well, if you ruin it, buddy, you're paying for it, and don't you forget it! On second thought, if you bring drink anywhere near my computer again, that's the last time you'll use it. Do you hear?"

Communication experts suggest a better way. Whenever you need to convey to someone that you are unhappy with their behavior and would like them to change, you want to convey your message in a way that runs the lowest risk of damaging the relationship. The experts suggest that the least risky message you could send in such a situation has three parts: (1) a non-judgmental description of the behavior that's bothering you; (2) your feelings about it; and (3) an explanation of the effect the behavior has on you. You might say, for example, "When water is brought around my computer, I get frightened, because a spill might ruin it, and I can't afford to buy another one." Or you might say, "When the cap is left off my pen, I get annoyed, because when I need it for my work, it's all dried out." Once you get used to formulating these kinds of messages, they don't seem so mechanical. For sure, they have a much better chance of drawing a positive response than an all-out attack.

All parents say things sometimes that they wish they could take back once they get their emotions under control. Although the damage has been done and healing may take awhile, one of the good things that can come of such mistakes is that they provide opportunities to apologize. Children don't need perfect parents. They do need parents who will model for them how to say "sorry" and make amends.

Hurtful, rude, insensitive, cruel, bullying, teasing words destroy relationships. Comments like, "How could you be so stupid!" "You'll never amount to anything!" "Sometimes I wish you'd never been born!" "Why can't you be more like your sister?" put up huge barriers to open communication. Messages that address the behavior rather than pass judgment on the person stand a better chance of being heard and prompting a desire to change in the other person.

Words that build people up, on the other hand, are soothing, encouraging, kind, thoughtful, loving words. Try some of these for starters: "Is there anything I can do to help you?" "You're doing such a great job! Keep it up!" "I'm so glad I'm your dad." "What you did for your grandmother was so thoughtful!" "If I could have chosen any child in the world to be mine, I could never have found one as special as you."

Words can start wars or promote peace, break down people and relationships, or build them up. What will your words do for your family today?

Good Fences
Make Good
Neighbors

"Whoever listens to me will live in safety and be at ease, without fear of harm."—*Proverbs 1:33*

Six-year-old Christopher loved football. He was so excited when his dad took him along to his first real game. They got there early and found their seats. Christopher was hungry, so Dad said they could get a snack before the game started. But first he needed to show Christopher something very important. "Son," he said, "football games can be quite long. You can get up and stretch your legs once in awhile, but the officials have rules about where you can go and where you cannot go. I want to show you just where those places are."

"You can go along our row of seats to the steps," Dad continued, taking Christopher by the hand and showing him the boundaries as they went. "Then you can walk up and down these steps, but you must watch carefully to make sure you don't bump into anyone. Now, do you see this bottom step? The football officials don't allow anyone who is not part of the game to go beyond this point. You might get in the way of the people in charge of the game. You see the step I am telling you that you can't go beyond, right?" Christopher nodded. "Okay," his dad went on. "So you can move about by yourself if you stay in the places we've talked about. If you don't, you'll have to stay seated unless I am with you. Is that clear?"

"Yes," Christopher affirmed.

"Good! Now, let's see if we can find that snack." Dad smiled.

Boundaries are very important. The American poet Robert Frost expressed this thought in a line in one of his best known poems. "Good fences make good neighbors," the old farmer in the poem said on many occasions. When a farmer puts a fence around his land, he may do so for a number of reasons.

- He may put it there to show other people the property lines that define the exact piece of ground that belongs to him.
- He may put it there to protect his family and belongings by discouraging trespassers and wild animals from coming onto his land.
- He may also put it there to protect his children and animals from wandering away from the "safety zone" he is working hard to provide.

Fences or walls establish very clear boundaries. When we set down behavioral boundaries for our children, there may or may not be visible markers. This makes it all the more important to make sure that children understand exactly where the boundaries are and what is required to stay within them. Dad laid out clear boundaries for Christopher at the football game. Christopher could go along their row of seats and down the aisle to the bottom step, but no further. Dad checked that Christopher knew exactly where the boundaries were so that there could be no misunderstanding. Finally, Dad made sure Christopher knew the consequences he would experience if he went beyond the area that had been marked out for him.

The boundaries were set, first of all, to protect Christopher. This was Christopher's first time at a football match, so he would have no way to know exactly what to expect or how to behave. Dad knew that if Christopher stepped off the bottom step onto the football pitch, he could easily cause a problem or get into trouble with one of the game officials, maybe even get hurt. Dad wanted to protect his son from an accident or from being embarrassed. The boundary was also there to make certain that the football game would not be disrupted by any fan interference. Dad established the boundary at the beginning so that he could enjoy the game and not have to worry about Christopher running off and getting into places where he shouldn't be.

The father in this story knew a lot about children. He knew his son would need to run about a bit and burn up some energy. He also knew the potential problems that might arise for a child attending a game for the first time. The boundary was fair and realistic. It allowed Christopher the space he needed to move about, but it established appropriate parameters to assure safety and enjoyment.

This wise father also knew that it's not enough to merely establish boundaries. He knew that it's absolutely predictable that children will routinely test them. Christopher was no exception. The boy soon grew bored waiting for the game to start and wanted to be up and about. He ran up the steps, then down the steps, stopping on the very bottom one. Then, turning to see if his dad were watching, he deliberately extended his leg into the forbidden space. Christopher needed to test the boundary. How important was it really for him not to run past the bottom step? What would happen if he did? What would his dad do?

It's important to remember that children cross boundaries for different reasons. Understanding some of these reasons can help us respond more appropriately when the line has been over-stepped.

Sometimes a boundary is crossed by accident. Christopher might have crossed the boundary by accident if he'd been running too fast and couldn't stop himself, or if he'd tripped over or been pushed by someone. Accidents happen. They happen to adults as well as to children. A child can be very confused if he's disciplined for something that he never intended to do because it happened accidentally.

Sometimes a boundary is crossed because of inexperience, or because we haven't explained things clearly enough or taught the child what to do. It's easy to assume a child knows what to do because they've seen us do it so many times. But it's too much to assume that they really know what is expected of them if we have not explained clearly and checked to see that the child has understood.

Sometimes a child will cross a boundary for attention. Christopher might step off the bottom step some time during the football match because Dad is so absorbed in the game that he is not responding to Christopher's needs. Perhaps he needs a drink or to go to the bathroom. If children are stepping over the boundaries we've set often, we need to ask ourselves if we're giving them the attention they need. Ask yourself, "Is disobedience the only way to get my attention?"

Sometimes a child will cross a boundary deliberately, just to test or challenge the boundary setters. Parents cannot afford to ignore this challenge. Kindly, but firmly, the boundary must be re-established, and the child must be allowed to experience appropriate consequences for over-stepping the established limit. This is the only way that children learn self-control and can be protected from the more serious consequences that boundary violations might bring upon them. One of the goals of discipline is to help the child understand why the boundaries are there, and why they are important.

When Dad saw Christopher on the bottom step extending his leg into the forbidden space, he got out of his seat and walked calmly down to the bottom step. There he bent down and showed Christopher how busy the officials were who were running up and down the edge of the pitch. He explained again how Christopher might get hurt or spoil the game if he stepped over the edge. Then he matter-of-factly reminded Christopher that if he did step off the bottom step, he would have to stay in his seat next to Dad.

As often as Christopher ventured to the bottom step and looked back to see what his dad would do if he stepped off, his dad repeated the same procedure. Finally Christopher grew weary of the process, resigned himself to the area marked out for him to move about, and became involved in watching the game. In the meantime he'd learned some important lessons:

- Dad means what he says.
- Dad loves me and wants me to enjoy the football match. That's why he gave me the "bottom step rule."
- I'm safest and happiest when I listen to my dad and do what he says.

An important part of growing up is to understand the wisdom of living within safe boundaries and choose to stay within them, even when adults are not looking over their shoulders. Think about the boundaries you've set in your home. What boundaries or rules do you have? Are they realistic for the ages, abilities and needs of your children? Are the rules and the consequences for violating them clearly understood by all? How often are the boundaries crossed? Why do you think the children are challenging them and you? Do the boundaries need to be moved or strengthened? And most importantly, do the children know the boundaries are there because you love them?

Discipline That
Leads to Life

"The corrections of discipline are the way to life." —*Proverbs 6:23*

Mrs. Murray was curious. "What was Tom doing sneaking along her back fence? Why wasn't he walking home from school along the road with the other boys?" Just then she saw him open the back gate, swing it around to the inside, and disappear behind it. "Strange!" she thought. A few minutes later he emerged and continued along the fence, looking like he was trying to make himself invisible. "What could he be up to?" she wondered.

Picking up a basket of wet clothes from the laundry, she opened the back door and called out. "Tom, is that you? Got time for some cookies after I get these clothes on the line? You could help me if you like. Take that rag there and wipe the lines down for me. I think I heard it raining in the night."

Tom looked like a cat caught with his paw in the goldfish bowl. "Oh, hello Mrs. M," he stammered. "I hope you're not mad at me for walking through your garden. Please don't call my dad. I can explain everything."

Mrs. M said nothing. She just passed Tom the clothespin bag. He began to hand clothespins to her two at a time like he'd done a dozen times before. "I must admit you had me a bit curious," Mrs. M broke the silence. "I couldn't figure out why you were walking out back all by yourself instead of down the road with your friends. Then you disappeared behind the gate. You know an old woman like me has to be on the lookout for excitement!"

Tom couldn't help but laugh. But for the young man, this really wasn't a laughing matter. "Well, look at me," he began in all seriousness. "Isn't it obvious why I couldn't be seen out on the road? You can't go out in public in these!" Tom lifted his eyes to meet Mrs. M's, confident she'd understand. It was the first time Mrs. M had paid any attention to Tom's pants. They seemed to fit okay; there was nothing odd about the color. "It's the bell bottoms, Mrs. M. Nobody wears bell bottoms these days," Tom went on.

"My dad got them on sale last week at such a good price he couldn't resist. He said I had to wear them to school because he can't take them back, and they're too good to throw away."

"And you couldn't bear to wear them in front of your friends, so you changed into your other pants on the way to school," Mrs. M guessed. "Just now you hid behind my gate to put your new pants back on before your father saw you, is that it?" Tom nodded. "Well, that certainly solves one mystery! Don't worry Tom, your secret's safe with me. But what will you do if your dad drops by the school one day or sees you in the schoolyard?" Tom hadn't thought that far. But he could well imagine what would happen if his dad knew what he had done.

When children disobey, parents' first impulse is often to move into disciplinary action. Perhaps it was Mrs. M's love for boys or lessons learned by hard experience as a parent that made her so wise. Maybe she was just a natural. But she was asking all the right questions. Child development specialists consider curiosity to be one of the best possible traits you can bring to parenthood. Much more often than not there is a logical reason for behavior that on the surface may appear to be defiance.

"Children's behavior," the experts like to say, "is purposeful." Usually there's an unmet need behind it. Before moving to disciplinary action, the first question we should be asking is the curiosity question: "I wonder what made them do that?" The answer may help us clear up the problem by simply meeting the needs behind the misbehavior. Tom needs not to be embarrassed in front of his friends. Perhaps your child needs a nap, something to eat, a hug and some of your attention, or reassurance you'll not be leaving the family like their friend's dad did last week. If parents move too quickly to discipline, they may never identify the real problem. In that case, the discipline is not likely to be effective and may even make matters worse.

Of course there are those times when children deliberately step over the line and violate clearly established boundaries. At such times, most parents understand that discipline is called for. However, the "how to" part of the discipline is more difficult. It may be helpful to think through the goals and objectives of discipline before considering the "how to's." An ancient writer of proverbs once said, "The corrections of discipline are the way to life." Discipline is about helping children learn to be responsible for their own actions and teaching them to put things right again when they've made a mistake. It is about helping kids back onto the road that leads to the good life after they've slipped into the ditch. So what kind of discipline is it that leads to life?

Disciplinary methods that allow children to learn from their mistakes and begin again with new opportunities to make better choices are much more effective than harsh punishments or the permissive avoidance of discipline all together. Most experts agree that a very effective method of discipline is the use of natural and logical consequences. When using this method, children learn by experiencing the consequences of their behavior. For example, if Brett leaves his bike out on the lawn and it gets stolen, his parents don't go out immediately to buy him a new one. Brett either has to do without a bike, or he has to work to earn money to replace the one that was lost. If Brittany consistently stays out with her friends beyond the agreed upon curfew, she's grounded for a week or two, then she may try again. If Sara spends all her clothes money on a bathing suit, she won't have money for the new skirt she's been looking at in the store window until her clothing allowance is available again.

This approach to discipline is flexible enough to accommodate different age and maturity levels. It allows for negotiation and compromise when differing circumstances warrant a change in the usual guidelines. It keeps the focus on the behavior that is unacceptable, rather than passing a negative judgment on the child as a person. It matches the magnitude of the consequences with the seriousness of the misbehavior. Thus the corrective measures have a better chance of being perceived by the child as fair and reasonable. This approach also allows the parent to tailor the consequences to the personality of a particular child. A very sensitive child may respond positively to something as simple as a talk with a parent, while some other children seem to have to learn the hard way. Most importantly, the use of natural and logical consequences emphasizes forgiveness, learning and opportunity to make better choices.

To be most effective, children need to know what the consequences of stepping out of bounds will be before they choose to misbehave. Rules should be few, but when they are broken, consequences should follow. Discipline can be all the more effective if the children have been included in deciding what the consequences for breaking a rule should be. Frequently, children will be harder on themselves than adults might have been.

Tracy mindlessly picked at a small snag in her best skirt until she had unraveled the threads into a big hole that couldn't be repaired. When Mom discovered it, she asked Tracy what she thought they ought to do about the problem. Tracy felt very badly about what she had done. "Mom, I think I should have to pay for a new one out of the money I've been saving to go to summer camp."

Mom was pleased with the way Tracy took responsibility for her behavior and her willingness to bear significant consequences. "I really think you learned from this experience, Tracy," Mom responded. "How about I pay half this time. That way you can still save enough by summertime to go to camp. I'm sure you won't make this mistake again."

When it comes to discipline, it's important to keep things in perspective. Most children behave well most of the time. One wonders why it's so easy to focus on mistakes and leave the good behavior unaffirmed. Children need encouragement. They need families who cheer them on from the sidelines and find every opportunity to let them know they believe the best about them. They will respond positively when their good behavior is reinforced with affirming words and actions. After all, discipline is not so much about teaching a child what's wrong as it about teaching them what's right!

Tasty  Smorgasbords

"Train a child in the way he should go, and when he is old he will not turn from it."—Proverbs 22:6

Alberto was sitting in the barber chair when a man entered with his teenaged son. The boy had shoulder-length hair while his father's hair was clipped short in a military cut. When one of the other barbers called the son to his chair, he asked the usual question, "What can I do for you today?" The boy responded, "Just a trim." Instantly the father was on his feet. With his face inches from the face of the barber, the father shouted: "I did not bring him in here for 'just a trim'! You, sir, are being paid for a hair *cut!*" The tension in the barbershop was so great at that moment, all conversation stopped in mid-sentence. No one made eye contact with anyone else. Everyone waited expectantly to see what the barber would do. It was a classic values collision between the generations.

High on the priority list of most parents is the hope that their children will buy into their values. Every parent has core beliefs and ideas that govern their choices and behaviors and which they hope their children will make part of their lives when they become adults. These ideas and beliefs that we hold most dear make their way into our value system through a variety of sources:

Personal preferences. Individuals have preferences related to their unique personalities. An extravert like Thomas typically prefers activities and careers that engage them with people. His more introverted brother Leslie would be more likely to place higher value on solo pursuits or those that require him to interact with one or two persons. Megan sticks with classic design in clothing, while her friend Melanie enjoys the variety in look and color that the new styles of each season provide. Al likes outdoor sports with strenuous physical activity; Rodney prefers table games. Lorrie likes chamber orchestra music, her husband likes folk tunes. These kinds of personal preferences are reflective of who we are as individuals. They are not matters of principle. One is not right and the other wrong. They are just various preferences among people who are different in personality and temperament from one another.

Culture. Nathan's family immigrated when he was just a child, so their cultural roots are in the homeland where parents play a large role in the choice of their children's marriage partners. Nathan would like to be married, but he remains single because he is unwilling to return to his former country to marry a wife of his parents' choosing. Every human being is born into a cultural milieu that leaves its mark on their life. For good or bad, we absorb into ourselves cultural ways of doing and thinking that have a profound influence over our lifestyle and decisions. Most parents, steeped as they are in their cultural background, place a high value on cultural traditions and mores. Mina's family culture has no problem with women taking the lead in the family in matters of business. So Mina's parents have a difficult time when Mina, who is an expert in financial matters, is left out entirely of the management of Mina's and her husband's new business. Conflicts often arise in families when one generation seeks to make changes in long-standing custom that no longer seems relevant or useful in the changing world in which they are growing up.

Religious beliefs. The core values held by many individuals grow out of their acceptance of the Bible or other religious teachings as God's guidebook for living. These values take on supreme importance in their lives because they believe they are from God and because they believe they will lead to the best quality of life human beings can know. Parents often have the most difficulty when their children challenge these core values which they believe to have higher than human origin.

On the way home from church, Shelley was more animated than usual about the morning's program in the teen division. She said that the leader had invited a real live auctioneer to be their guest. Only a few of the kids had ever been to an auction, but most everyone had seen one on T.V. or in a movie somewhere. He told them how he had gone to a special school to learn how to talk fast and get the best price for each of his clients' wares. He gave them tips on how to shop at an auction and bid wisely to get the most for your money.

Then the teacher announced that an auction was about to begin right there in class. Anyone who would like to participate was given $1000 in pretend currency. On the auction block were things like "a dream vacation for two in Paris," "a marriage partner who would love you for a lifetime," "a job at the top of the ladder in your chosen career," "good health," "season tickets for your favorite football team," "a year's study abroad," etc. As the auctioneer brought each item to the block, the kids bid for their favorites until their money was gone. Pranov spent all he had on "good health," while James nursed his disappointment over the loss of the season tickets. Despite the auctioneers tips, he had really not planned his purchasing and got caught up in the excitement of bidding on other items. Shelley's parents were keenly interested in her selections, recognizing immediately that they provided important insights into their daughter's emerging value system.

The question on Shelley's parents' minds as they talked later about what Shelley had said was "What can we do to increase the chances Shelley will want to buy our values?" Here are a few answers you might want to consider:

1. Define your target. Roland discovered only at the end of an archery class that he had been missing the bull's eye, at least in part, because he needed glasses! Parents who want to increase the likelihood their children will buy their values will need to think through exactly what values it is that they most want to convey to their children.

2. Live by the values you teach. It has been said that children do not learn values, they imitate people. While teaching is an important part of values transmission, it will have a much greater impact if alongside there is a life well-lived.

3. Build strong relationships. Children buy values from people they like and whom they know like them. In the end, a warm, positive relationship with your children creates the best likelihood that children will buy your values.

4. Adopt a parenting style that combines love and limits. Research is clear that two factors are common in families where the kids buy values from the family in which they grew up. In these families, there is much love, warm, open communication, and fun. There are also age-appropriate limits, and agreed-upon consequences that will follow if these limits are breeched.

5. Give your children room to be themselves. Children are not clones; they are unique individuals. Particularly in the teen years, they will need to separate from parents to develop their own unique identities and system of values. This differentiation is essential in their growth toward full maturity as a responsible adult. The challenge of parenthood is to help our children become separate selves without having to reject the most important core values of the family to do so.

6. Discuss core values in the context of daily life. The news, happenings in the lives of families and friends, your own life experience and that of your children offer a wealth of opportunity for you to open dialogue with your children about your most important values. While real life provides many teachable moments, scenarios opened by a television show, a movie, a book someone in the family is reading, or a case study presented to the family for the express purpose of opening discussion on a particular value can also lead to the kinds of discussions that give everyone in the family opportunity to think through what they believe and why.

7. Make your values winsome. Roger Dudley spent his research career seeking to understand why some young people espouse the core values of their families and why others turn their backs on what their parents affirm. His conclusion?

I like to think of value transmission as a huge smorgasbord where all the tempting dishes of competing values are displayed. Here the youth will eventually get to choose the items that are most appealing to them. And which will they choose? Those that are most colorful and attractive, most delectable, most tasty! It is not our responsibility to force our values upon our young people. It is our responsibility to model our values so attractively that these youth cannot help seeing that they are vastly superior to the competition, and will freely choose them.[1]

What can you do today to make your values smorgasbord look irresistible?

ENDNOTES

1 Roger L. Dudley, *Passing On the Torch* (Hagerstown, MD: Review and Herald Publishing Association, 1986), 117.

Your Mommy, But
More Than Your
Mommy

"Oh Lord, . . . teach us how to bring up the boy who is to be born." —Judges 13:8

It's a girl!" exclaimed the midwife, "and she looks just like you!" Moments later Sophie was handed a tiny bundle in a white blanket. She looked at her daughter—red faced, with damp wisps of hair sticking to her head, crying and looking exhausted. Sophie couldn't help laughing outloud. The midwife was definitely right. After ten hours of labor, mother and daughter did look just alike!

The moment was very precious, each of them seeing the other for the first time. Then, without warning, Sophie's euphoria gave way to panic. During what season of temporary insanity had she and Martin decided to become parents? Oh, it wasn't as though this baby wasn't planned. The two of them had spent nine months preparing for this day. But they'd been so busy making sure everything was ready for the baby at home that they hadn't thought much about what it would mean to be a parent. There's nothing like holding your newborn in your arms to bring the full weight of parenting responsibility down hard on your shoulders.

Parenting can be a wild emotional ride. Moms and dads feel relieved every time the baby does something that the books say he should. At least he's "normal." They celebrate the day she learns to walk, then spend the next year worrying about her falling, climbing and getting into the wrong things. Sometimes parenting feels like one long string of anxieties. Parental burnout has become a very real phenomenon. With all the focus on children's needs, one very important parenting rule of thumb is often overlooked. It reminds us that when parents take care of themselves, they will have much more to give to their families than when they are emotionally drained, intellectually and relationally deprived or physically exhausted.

Some parenting seasons are more demanding than others because of the developmental challenges of children at a given age. Matthew and Michelle remember the first couple of years with their twins. They made jokes about how sleep deprivation threatened sanity, but there was a lot of truth behind the laughs. Pat and Stephanie coasted into early adolescence with Jeremy, wondering what all the fuss about parenting teenagers was all about. Then puberty struck, and seemingly overnight they began to appreciate book titles like *I Wanna Be Sedated: Thirty Writers on Parenting Teenagers* and *Suddenly They're 13: Or the Art of Hugging a Cactus*. Other parental seasons are complicated by external changes impacting the family, such as a move, a natural disaster, parental job loss, serious illness or war. Recognizing the predictability of such seasons can help you pace yourself for a successful finish and ask for help when you need it.

With three young children under six, Debbie was struggling. It seemed her life consisted of nothing more than chores and children, whichever pressed harder for her attention at the moment. No sooner had she cleaned a room than the children had it littered. As fast as she made a meal, someone was hungry again. Before long she felt as if there was nothing left of her. She was just the mommy drudge, with nothing but toddler prattle in her vocabulary and nothing but work on her agenda. One day in a brief lull, she sat down with a cold drink and made a list of all the things she would really like to do. She was so ready to reconnect with her unique personhood and with the outside world. She was also a realist, so her list wasn't long! Call Jan for a long chat. Finish that cross-stitch. Read *The Big Year!* (She was a bird lover, and if she couldn't be free to participate in the annual competition for the most birds seen in a year in North America, she could at least enjoy the experience vicariously.) She decided then and there to give herself 15 minutes a day to do something on her list. It wasn't much, but it would be a start.

Joanne remembers the day she made the momentous decision to shut the door behind her when she went into the bathroom. Since the children had been born, they had followed her around like puppies. She had given up the most basic of privacies. Today would be different she told herself. While she was in there, the phone rang. As there was a portable phone within reach, she answered cheerily. "I can almost hear you smiling," her friend teased on the other end of the line. "Have you put all the little darlings down for a long nap this early in the morning?"

"No," laughed Joan. "I have locked myself in the bathroom. I said to myself this morning, 'Today we pee alone!' I'm feeling like a new person already!"

Kenton worked in a busy office just five minutes from his home. There seemed no time or space between the onslaught of questions and needs that faced him at the office and another round of the same that met him when he arrived home. A few minutes of space was all he needed between one barrage and the next, he told himself. But it was hard to shut himself away from a wife and four little ones who were so excited that he was home! One day Kenton decided to walk home from the office. He took the long way around, down a quiet road where he could unwind and let go of all the issues at work before he reached the house. When he walked through his front door only a few minutes later than usual, he found he could respond much better to his family's needs, having first taken care of his own.

Nancy remembers the day she made an announcement to her children: "I love being your mommy," she proclaimed with enthusiasm. "But did you know that I am more than your mommy? I am Daddy's wife, I am the leader of the parent group at your school, and I am Nancy who likes to read and paint pictures. Right now I want to be Nancy and read my book for awhile. Can you play by yourselves for a few minutes and give me a little time to be Nancy?"

Perhaps your children are grown and you have time to give to a child. Is there a single parent or a struggling couple in your neighborhood or circle of acquaintances that could use a little time for themselves, perhaps tickets to a concert or a gift certificate for dinner-for-two at a nice restaurant with babysitting included?

John and Melody loved each other. There just wasn't much time or energy for romance anymore. Everyday seemed a repeat of the day before. Get up. Get dressed. Eat breakfast. Drop kids at school. Go to work. Come home. Eat supper. Help with homework. Tuck kids in bed. Watch news. Go to bed. Money was tight, so getting away for the weekend seemed out of the question. One day John read an article about marriage that said the relationship between husband and wife is the cornerstone relationship in the family. As goes the marriage, so goes the family, the author said. The article told the story of a man who planned a surprise getaway for his wife. John got a lot of ideas from the story that really didn't need to cost that much. John had never really thought of himself as a romantic, but from that day he determined to surprise Melody big time.

He found a quaint bed and breakfast less than an hour away and made reservations. He arranged for Melody's best friend to pick the kids up at school on Friday and keep them for the weekend. He planned the events of the weekend with just enough aforethought and just enough room for spontaneity to be more than a little pleased with himself. He packed a bag for both of them, getting one of her friends to help him choose outfits she would like and that suited each occasion in his weekend itinerary. Melody was blown away. John said it was like falling in love all over again.

Someone once said to a room full of dads, "The best gift you can give your children is to love their mother." The same could be said to mothers about fathers. It's true not only because children thrive in an atmosphere of love and security, but also because parents who tend to their own relationship have a reservoir of love and security from which to draw in times of stress and overload. Such parents are less likely to turn to their children inappropriately to meet their adult needs. And when their years of active parenting in the home are over, they will have a life together that transcends their parental responsibilities. What's more, their children will have seen a marriage close-up that will be worth emulating. It's a JumpStart you can't buy over the counter.